BE A MASTER® OF YOUR REALITY

AUTHENTICALLY MANIFEST YOUR DESIRES

Dr. Theodoros Kousouli

A Personal Empowerment Book

Kousouli Enterprises
Los Angeles, CA

Copyright © 2018 by Theodoros Kousouli D.C., CHt.

All rights reserved. No part of this book may be reproduced or utilized in any form or by any means, electronic or mechanical including photocopying, recording, or by any information storage and retrieval system, without permission in writing from the author and publisher, except for the inclusion of brief quotations in a review with proper credit cited.

The BE A MASTER® BOOK SERIES (http://www.BEAMASTER.com) trademarked brand and work is Copyright of Dr. Theodoros Kousouli.

The KOUSOULI® mark and the Kousouli® Method 4R Intervention health system are registered trademarks of Theodoros D. Kousouli D.C., CHt. and Kousouli Enterprises.

Heartfelt gratitude to the following for their contributions:
Editor: Latasha Doyle
Covers: Shutterstock; Stockforliving
Dr. Kousouli Photo Back Cover: Matthew A. Cooke
Layout coordinator: Gustavo Martinez

ISBN: 978-0997627688   Softcover
ISBN: 978-0997627695   Epub
ISBN: 978-0998958408   Kindle

Library of Congress Control Number: 2017906292

Kousouli Enterprises
P.O. Box 360494
Los Angeles, CA 90036

Printed in the United States of America

CONTENTS

Disclaimer vii

Introduction xi
   A Note on the Layout of This Book xiv
   Your In-Vision Board xiv

Chapter One: Getting to Know Our Authentic Selves 1
   Body & Physicality 2
      In-Vision Board Exercise [My Childhood] 4
      In-Vision Board Exercise [My Young Adulthood] 5
   Mind & Emotions 6
      In-Vision Board Exercise [My Mental and Emotional Fields] 8
      In-Vision Board Exercise [My Kind of Relationship] 9
   Spirit & Soul 10
      In-Vision Board Exercise [My Spiritual Self] 11

Chapter Two: Focusing on Physical Authenticity 13
   2.1 Personal Health 13
      In-Vision Board Exercise [My New Self-Style] 14
   Personal Health Tips 1 - 38 15
      In-Vision Board Exercise [My New Body] 19

Chapter Three: Clearing Our Mental Space To Make Way For Authenticity . . . 37
   3.1 Creating Mental Space 37
   Creating Mental Space Tips 1 - 11 38
      In-Vision Board Exercise [My Dream State] 41
      In-Vision Board Exercise [My Personal Home Space] 43
      In-Vision Board Exercise [People I Admire] 48
   3.2 Mental Manifestation 49
   Mental Manifestation Tips 1 - 9 50

    Debt Elimination Exercise..55
        In-Vision Board Exercise [My Financial Status]..............63
    Mental Manifestation Tips 10 - 13..............................64
        In-Vision Board Exercise [My Perfect Career]................65
        In-Vision Board Exercise [My Perfect Transportation].......66
        In-Vision Board Exercise [A Productive Day in My Life]......70

Chapter Four: Connecting With Our Authentic Spirit 71

4.1 Life Traumas for Neutralization 71
    KNER® Neutralization Exercise [My Life Story Work Sheet].............73

4.2 Divine Solutions Through the Hand 75

4.3 Locate Negative Vibes [Aura Energy Exercise]................80

4.4 Recognize and Remove Negative Vibes and Negative People 88

4.5 Avoid, Disengage, and Grow Your Positive Posse 90

4.6 Meet like-minded positive people at workshops and seminars 91

Chapter Five: Daily Acts of Self Care 93
    Self care Tips 1 - 24 93

Chapter Six: Random Acts of Kindness 103
    Random acts of kindness 1 - 8 103

Chapter Seven: Novelty Keeps Us Young 107
    Novelty Tips 1 - 15 107

The Beginning, Not The End 115

Conclusion 117

About the Author 119

Note:

This life transformation tool, using the Kousouli® Method is best used together with the previous works in the BE A MASTER® Series (BeAMaster.com) by Dr. Theodoros Kousouli. However, it can still be used on its own to help you in your personal journey.

This workbook is meant to be used as an active journal for the reader to help facilitate a new perspective of living over the next six to twelve months and bring awareness to current challenges which need immediate attention. It is highly suggested the written printed version be used to complete the activities herein; otherwise a blank lined notebook and poster board (to complete the activities) can be used to accompany the digital version of this book.

Be a Master® of Your Reality

Life Changing Products · Books · Seminars · Empowerment Audios · Get on the Newsletter!

Connect with Dr. Kousouli, www.DrKousouli.com and on all Social Media Platforms

@DrKousouli #DrKousouli #KousouliMethod

You Will Also Enjoy Dr. Kousouli's Other Published Works Available Now from Major Retailers:

BE A MASTER® OF MAXIMUM HEALING
How to Lead a Healthy Life Without Limits
- Holistic Solutions for over 60 Diseases to Help You and Your Loved Ones Heal!

BE A MASTER® OF PSYCHIC ENERGY
Your Key to Truly Mastering Your Personal Power
- Uncover and Amplify Your Hidden Psychic Abilities to Change Your Life!

BE A MASTER® OF SEX ENERGY
Hypnotize Your Partner for Love and Great Sex
- Build a Stronger Bond with Your Lover(s) Using Subconscious Science!

BE A MASTER® OF SUCCESS
Dr.Kousouli's 33 Master Secrets to Achieving Your Dreams
- Solid Success Principles You can Apply Right Now to Empower Your Life!

BE A MASTER® OF SELF IMAGE
Dr.Kousouli's 33 Master Secrets to Living Healthier, Happier and Hotter
- Simple Holistic Tips & Tricks for More Weight Loss and Body Benefit to You!

BE A MASTER® OF SELF LOVE
Dr.Kousouli's 33 Master Secrets to Loving Your Extraordinary Life
- Overcome Bullying, Abuse, Depression and Build Massive Self-Esteem & Self-Love!

If you would like to share your story of how Dr. Kousouli's books, audios or seminars have impacted your life for the better, we would love to hear from you! (Messages are screened by staff and forwarded when appropriate.)

For A Free Gift from Dr. Theo Kousouli visit www.FreeGiftFromDrTheo.com

LEGAL DISCLAIMER

This publication is for informational purposes only. The material presented herein denotes the views of the author as of the date of press. The material and ideas provided herein are believed to be truthful and complete, based on the author's best judgment and experience, formed from the available data at the time of publication. Because of the speed by which conditions and information change, the author reserves the right to amend and update his opinions at any time based upon the new data and circumstances. While every effort has been made to provide complete, accurate, current, and reliable information within this publication, no warranties of any kind are expressed or implied. The publisher, author, and all associated parties involved with this publication assume no responsibility for errors, inaccuracies, oversights, or conflicting interpretations of the content herein. The author and publisher do not accept any responsibility for any liabilities resulting from the use of this information. Readers acknowledge that the author is not engaging in rendering guarantees of income or outcome of any kind in connection with using any methods, techniques, tips, suggestions, or information stated or implied. Any perceived results of the material's use can vary greatly per case and individual circumstance. Mention of any persons or companies in this book does not imply that they endorse this book, its content, or the author, and similarly the author does not endorse them. Any supposed slights of specific establishments, corporations, organizations, peoples, or persons are unintended.

You should consult your own chiropractor, acupuncturist, herbalist, naturopath, hypnotherapist, or other holistic doctor(s) in combination with sound medical advice. Readers are cautioned to first consult with proper health professionals about their individual circumstances on any matter relating to their health and personal well-being, prior to taking any course of action. The author is not a licensed medical doctor or psychiatrist and the ***information provided in this book should not be construed as personal, medical, or psychiatric advice or instruction***. All readers or users of the information herein, who fail to consult proper health experts, assume the risk of any and all injuries.

The contents of this book and the information herein have not been evaluated or approved by the Food and Drug Administration for the treatment or cure of any disease, disorder, syndrome, or ailment mentioned herein.

This book is dedicated to the limitless ones who show us the "I'm Possible" within the impossible.

"It is possible for ordinary people to choose to be extraordinary."

~ Elon Musk

INTRODUCTION

Are you bored with an ordinary monotonous life? Do you wake up every morning to do the same thing you did yesterday? Are you feeling like your life is just a series of events that you don't have much control over? Do you wish you had more excitement in your existence? Do you desire a more authentic life – one that you *yearn* to wake up for each day?

I know the feeling, and have been right where you are today.

Despite being a successful doctor in Beverly Hills, CA, my path to get here was not always clear. I went through a variety of struggles, from bullying in high school to semi-paralysis from a pool accident as a late teen. After going to college, I had to learn to adapt to my new (parent-free) environment and was opened up to a whole new world. Without my desire to learn the art and science of chiropractic care and spread my wings beyond Southern NJ, I would have been like many - stuck in a small-town bubble for the rest of my life. I remember having to make a choice, and that choice changed the course of my life for the better.

But even after all that growth, I still had one massive challenge preventing me from living life to the fullest.

The famous American writer, Mark Twain once said, "The two most important days in your life are the day you were born, and the day you find out why." October 5, 2005. I will never forget that day. I remember it vividly, as anyone in my position would. "*You have about eight months to live if we don't get your aortic valve replaced. Your heart will give out and then you'll internally bleed to death.*" It does not sink in - at first - when you're told that you might die soon.

Time speeds up, as if racing you to see if you can catch up.

Life was already stressful at this point in my life, with relationships, board exams, and mounting bills. But now, terror gripped me. Now, that innocent little heart murmur I was born with, that gave me three heartbeats instead of two, was about to go on permanent strike. I was still too young for my heart to be taking a final lap around the track, and I had not done all the things in life I desired to do yet.

After many exhausting nights of deep thought, I finally made peace with the fact I had to go through with the surgery. Before I knew it, the surgery date came and I was prepped and put into my requisite gown. I kissed my family goodbye and watched them disappear into the waiting room, as my mortality was becoming clearer by the second. "*I might never see them again,*" I thought to myself as I was wheeled down the cold hospital hallway to the operating room for what seemed like forever. I quietly started to pray. In desperation and mounting anger, I was beginning to lose my faith but, like most folks facing possible death, I decided to make a deal with God.

Up to this point in my life, I realized that I'd lived too selfishly and egotistically. I took too much for granted - my family, my friends, my time, my purpose - my whole life. What a waste it would be to let this life go without making something more of the gifts and talents I'd been given. I remember praying, *"God, If you want me to come back – And yes, I do want to come back - I will dedicate my time to serving you through helping others. Let me know you are with me when I ask, and when people ask for help, let me be able to give it to them through your grace. But please, if you want me to open my eyes and come back to continue this life, please make it easier for me so that I don't have to struggle like I used to. God, I want to feel love. I want to know what love is - real love. If you agree to all this, then I want to live and fulfill the highest purpose you have for me here."*

With those last words in my mind, I saw the anesthesiologist's hand place the mask over my face as I dropped into rest. I had finally let go and surrendered myself, as I allowed my soul much needed inner peace.

Dedication to Serving Others

I made it through that surgery, healing in just two months rather than the assumed 6-month recovery, thanks to my commitment to healing myself (along with my mother's excellent Greek food). 11 years later however, I was forced to face a second surgery to replace the valve that had been given to me at 28. I have fully recovered from that second surgery as I write this book, again thanks to my excellent surgeon, my commitment to natural healing and recovery through the Kousouli® Method, my chiropractic care, and the people in my life who love me.

But most of all, my ability to heal stems from a commitment I made a long, long time ago to push on. To live that life I had told God I would live when I was 28 and terrified. And while I still have big challenges that bring about self-discovery, I know that God has helped me through these things because I have helped myself. I choose to push on – no matter what. I thought, "I've come to a point in my life that, if I did not write this or my other books, it would be a shame. A huge life potential lost." All that I have been through, all that I have done, has been for a reason. It was to help others, like yourself, choose to maximize your life here.

We know that life is too short to just be bored, get sick, and die. That is not our purpose on this planet. Many do get lost in the tumultuous chaos of life's challenges and they lose focus of the big picture. Our purpose is to look within, find our innermost talents that bring us and the world joy and to live every day at the highest vibration of love expression that we can. And so I was asked by my readers to write a book on finding your inner joy, a book on finding and being your authentic self.

How do we change our lives one day at a time to make sure that we live life to the fullest? Obviously, I don't ask everyone to have my experiences, so how do I show people they can love their lives and change their experiences if they are not happy with them currently? The answer was simple: I can give people the tools they need to live a life that is fully authentic. An authentic life that is theirs; their own rules, their own experiences, their own unconditional love of life, and their own connection to God, whatever that means for them.

I desire to give you ammunition to make your life easier and even more amazing and let you know that, if I can do it, you can, too. In this book, you'll find something that you can try each day if you wish to do so. No pressure, no rules. I don't believe in that. I believe if you show someone their truth, the rest will unfold naturally. Their spirit will move them into daily repetitive self-discovery. You can jump around the book, flip pages, browse, come back to things. You don't have to do these things in order and you don't have to do them at all – but where is the fun in that? Have fun with this book; live a little.

And if I ever see you in one of my seminars, I will show you how to further live your life to the fullest personally. Looking back at my life thus far, I see the steps I took to get here, and this book will give you some simple, exciting ideas to radically change your life for the better. Imagine if you did all of them! Better yet, imagine if you didn't stop at this book; what if you could change your whole life from the inside out, from now until the day you shed your physical body and return to full spirit again? Don't end your education and ability to grow with just one tool or piece of information.

A wealth of knowledge awaits you at www.BEAMASTER.com so you can fully become a Master of Your Own Life! Let's get started!

A note on the formatting of this book….

Before we really dive into the tips you'll find in this book, I desire to take a moment to discuss the layout. Think of this book as your own personal transformation journal. It's a book you're personalizing over the next six to twelve (or more) months. The first part of this book will discuss your life as you live it now. We'll address your current situation, what you like about your life, and what you cannot wait to change. Most of all, we'll see where you desire to create authenticity.

In the second part of this book, you'll see tips for increasing your overall life satisfaction and your authentic experience. These tips are broken into sections that focus on your:

- Body
- Mind
- Spirit

This makes it easier for you to pick tips that are most relevant to where you are in life (or where you are physically) so that you can find what you're capable of incorporating into your life right now.

But you'll also notice that, in between these sections, there are full blank pages. What I ask you to do with these blank pages is to create an "In-vision" board inspired by each section.

What is an In-vision board?

The In-vision board is a powerful tool you can use to manifest your desires and dreams. To manifest these goals, the creator of the board uses emotional feeling, the physical senses of vision and touch, as well as the nonphysical 6th sense through thought and imagination. All of these senses (and the energy they emit) will combine to help you harness the Law of Attraction and the Law of Vibration to create a truly authentic life for yourself. You can literally help attract your desires to you and eventually change your life path to a more prosperous and authentic one.

NOTE: These are not the only two laws that govern your life. There are many more which are discussed in depth in BE A MASTER® OF PSYCHIC ENERGY.

How do I build a powerful In-Vision Board?

This has been built-in to this book as you go through the exercises and read the content. All you will need is this physically printed book (If you are using a digital tablet to read it, put all the content on a poster board), a pencil or pen, scissors, glue, favorite magazines with ads and images of things you desire, and a quiet place with no distractions. The most important thing is to have fun and feel really good about what you're going to paste on each board or In-Vision pages.

This book serves as your In-vision board (visualize within your mind's eye – 'inner' vision). This book is your private area of creation and the energy you put onto the boards will manifest for you depending on your focus, dedication, enactment of Universal laws, and belief system. Be sure to create in a place of no distraction or negative criticism. Keep this book (containing your boards within the pages) for constant reference, and view your In-vision boards frequently.

Include places to travel to or new career paths you desire to try. You can cut out pictures of specific landmarks you'd like to see or new food you desire to eat. You may also cut out pictures of people laughing or snuggling with their loved ones, which could represent a loving relationship you seek.

Your board may contain both pictures and words. You may cut out magazine ads, photos, and even letters or word phrases for your poster board. You may put any combination of words and pictures together. You may group pictures in clumps or spread them out as you wish. There are no rules for whatever it is you desire. You do not have to finish an entire board in one sit-down session, either. I recommend reading each section and then creating your In-vision board as you browse through your materials – there is no sense in rushing to find what feels good!

When you've found images you would like to cut out, feel what it's like to own that item (or experience); what it would be like to live your life with that item (or feeling) as yours. Feel nothing but joy and happiness in your heart, your soul, and your being as you put glue on the back of the pictures, thanking the universe *for each desire*. Continue this step until each board is filled with items, ideas, thoughts, words, and anything else you desire to bring into your life experience. Your boards are now complete!

How does the In-vision board actually work?

The world you currently live in and experience is the total collection of your past ideas, thoughts, belief systems, cultural and traditional expectations, physical actions, and deep emotional feelings. These are invested over time to give you exactly what you are experiencing now. If you change all those aspects, given time, you will have a new combination of reality you will be living. Knowing this, and taking responsibility for the process, should get you very excited! You can radically change your life with the processes in this book.

The reason I ask you to be discerning with your In-vision board's images and text is that *powerful emotion can manifest your wishes in reality.* This means that if you're just sort of ambivalent to the images you're cutting out, the Law of Attraction will be ambivalent to your wishes.

The Latin word for '*desire*' means 'of or from the Father/God/King/Sire.' When you flip through the magazines and find things that you desire to bring into your reality, claim them as yours just before you cut them out to place on your board. Then, I recommend keeping your boards with you so you can look at them each and every day.

Close your eyes as you envision each still image becoming a moving picture as you play out the scenario in your mind - the way it will be when you acquire it. Give thanks to the Universe with complete gratitude as you envision your life with that item and witness your desires fulfilled. Be sure not to wish that you will have it or hope for it in the future, but instead think and feel the joy as if it is yours now. Starting and ending your day on a creative note with joy will magnetize the item(s) or situation(s) closer to you.

Allowing yourself time and space to put the images of your desires in this book enables you to construct a roadmap for your next possible growth cycle. This exercise allows you to invoke feelings of fulfillment as you tangibly attach the image with the idea of 'manifestation' in this current dimension of reality, thus experiencing that version of having; not lacking. When you see results start to manifest, this will be your 'proof' that you have Divine ability to steer your life as you like.

Keep this book close as you start on your new journey

This book is your private area of creation, and the energy you put onto the pages are meant to manifest for you, not others. So be sure to create in a place of no distraction and no negative criticism. Keep this book for future reference and view your In-vision boards frequently throughout your day. Even a quick glance for a few seconds here and there will refresh your mind and energy field to move towards attracting your desires. As you begin creating your boards within this book itself, you will start to see this book as the very source of creation, positivity, and manifestation. How amazing – to be able to keep the source of your hopes and dreams right in your backpack!

CHAPTER ONE:
GETTING TO KNOW OUR AUTHENTIC SELVES

The basic definition of the word "authentic" is real; genuine. Let me ask you a question, one that might make you uncomfortable: Are you real? Are you genuine? I don't mean a real *human*, of course, you are flesh and blood. But I mean are you a *real* person with *genuine* feelings, desires, and experiences?

The opposite of authentic is often unreliable, counterfeit, *fake.* Do you feel like a fake? Do you feel like you wake up each day living someone else's life – or living the way someone else told you to live? Many times, we follow trends, do what our friends are doing, follow our parents' aspirations for us, and live our lives "the way we think we should" - without ever considering how we feel about it or even why we're following the current.

When I say authentic self, I mean the real you; me; *us.* The original creation of love and light that our creator made us be. We re-create versions of this original image which was and is made in the likeness of our creator. However, over time, a lot of sludge gets on that very crystal clear image of self and, before we know it, our direction in life takes a turn for the worse. Much like if your car had no windshield wipers, over time, you won't be able to see where you are going!

This book, as well as the others in the BE A MASTER® series, helps clear the windshield to help you excel and master life from all angles. The exercises in here are very effective and, if taken seriously, can open up a whole new world for you. Take a long look at your life and help you re-discover your authentic self. Maybe you'll see things you don't like along the way, things you don't necessarily love about yourself. As you go through the exercises the book will shed light on some situations and then give you the tools you need to turn your life around.

First, you're going to ask yourself a series of questions and fill in the blanks below each one.

BODY & PHYSICALITY

1. What is your style? Do you have unique clothing, accessories, or features that you love to show off?
___
___
___

Is this look really "you"? What do you desire it to look like if not?
___
___
___

2. What is your current state of health? Is it ideal for you? Why or why not?
___
___

What do you need to change to experience authentic health?
___
___

3. How do you feel about your body? Do you have a positive body image? Why or why not?
___
___

4. What do you need to change for this part of your life to become truly authentic?
___
___

5. Detail your financial situation. Are you mostly satisfied with how you earn, consume, save, or invest your money?
___
___

6. What do you desire from your money in the future? How can you have an authentic relationship with money? Do you need money, or does money need you? What is your prevailing attitude about money?
_____
_____
_____
_____
_____

7. Have you traveled? Are you excited for your next adventure, or do you just talk about traveling *some day*?
_____
_____

8. If travel is an authentic wish of yours, how can you make it happen?
_____
_____

9. As a child what did you desire to become when you "grew up"?
_____
_____

10. What personal trait or characteristic do you like most about yourself?
_____
_____
_____

11. What talents do you possess or wish to develop?
_____
_____

MY CHILDHOOD

IN-VISION BOARD
CUT & PASTE PAGE

॰६॰६॰६

Look through old albums or photo memories. Cut out happy photos of you as a newborn, infant, toddler, or young child and put them here on these pages. Make a collage of the little loving soul that entered the world and notice the tenderness, the innocence, the joy and gleam of opportunity in your eyes. We all come into this world knowing we have everything we need to be happy as we embark on learning everything fresh from the start.

॰६॰६॰६

MY YOUNG ADULTHOOD

IN-VISION BOARD
CUT & PASTE PAGE

ഏഏഏ

Look through old albums or photo memories. Cut out happy photos of you as a young adult before any challenges or difficulties presented themselves. Focus on happy times and moments of triumph. If you do not have photos available, start cutting out things from magazines that remind you of your childhood. You can also print out things from the internet and glue them here. You may fill the whole page or overlap photos; add what you feel is relevant.

ഏഏഏ

MIND & EMOTIONS

1. Describe your environments, both at home and at work (or school). How do you feel when you're there?

_____
_____
_____

2. What do you need to change for this part of your life to become truly authentic to who you really are?

_____
_____
_____

3. What does your social life look like? Who are your closest, truest friends? How do you feel with them? Are they a positive influence on you?

_____
_____
_____

4. What do you need to change for this part of your life to become truly authentic? Which friends could be replaced with more positive ones?

_____
_____
_____

5. If you are in a relationship, how does it make you feel? What future do you see with this person(s)?

_____
_____
_____

6. If you are single, what is your ideal relationship? What are you looking for in an authentic partner? What adjectives describe this person's character?
_____
_____

7. Whether you're single or in a relationship, ask yourself: Am I/will I be authentic with this other person? Have you been authentic with past lovers?
_____
_____

8. What do you do for fun? What do you just *love* doing? Is it something that other people love, or is it something you hide from others? Do others mock you for what you find entertaining?
_____
_____

9. How can you become authentic in your pleasures and entertainment?
_____
_____

10. Name your current level of success – however you measure that. Are you happy with your career or progress in life?
_____
_____
_____

11. Is this "success" your own definition of success – or someone else's?
_____
_____

MY MENTAL AND EMOTIONAL FIELDS

IN-VISION BOARD
CUT & PASTE PAGE

Look through magazines or get images from the internet that depict how you would like your mental and emotional fields to be. Are you currently cloudy or foggy and wish to be a bit clearer? Are you desiring your mental and emotional outlook be more vibrant or brighter? Are your emotions too heavy and do you wish to seek a lighter nature for yourself? Cut and paste, creating the optimum scenario for how you wish to feel. Keep your images positive, light, and happy - just as you wish to experience your new-found life.

MY KIND OF RELATIONSHIP

IN-VISION BOARD
CUT & PASTE PAGE

Look through magazines and cut out the kind of relationship your soul seeks. Not the type of relationship your outer, superficial, unauthentic self wants; concentrate on your soul's desires. Do you desire to be respected? Adored? Loved? Do you seek someone who reciprocates love? Maybe someone who shares a love for art, poetry, and travel? Be sure to really think about this one before pasting down your ideal mate. You may wish to save this part for later and come back to it after you have gone through more of the book to discover yourself. Sometimes, before you can see the person you desire to attract, you have to find out who *you* are first. We do tend to attract the level of partner we can handle and they are usually at the same level we are. This means that the more we work on ourselves, the better our understanding of our authentic self will be, and the more authentic a match in vibration will be. If you're not in a good state of mind right now, you may desire to develop yourself further before you attract the wrong person. Complete this page when you feel you can authentically put down the person that best vibrationally matches what you deserve.

SPIRIT & SOUL

1. What are your spiritual beliefs?
_____
_____

2. Do you meditate or pray? What do you meditate on or pray for?
_____
_____

3. Are your beliefs or spiritual behaviors a result of your own exploration and authentic experience with God? Did someone else influence you into your current spiritual journey? (Ex. Church, parents, friends)
_____
_____

4. If you don't consider your current spiritual journey to be authentic, what *does* an authentic one look & feel like to you?
_____
_____

5. What does your soul feel like? Is it heavy or light? What does it desire?
_____
_____
_____

6. Does your soul reflect who you truly are? Are you holding back your soul from your outer self?
_____
_____
_____

MY SPIRITUAL SELF

IN-VISION BOARD
CUT & PASTE PAGE

Look through magazines or get images from the internet that depict how you would like your spiritual self to be. Is religion a large part of your life? Are you more spiritual than religious? Are you seeking a better connection with the Divine? On this page, fill it with what you would like your connection to God to be or, if you don't yet have a relationship with God, the relationship you wish to create. For some people, connecting to God starts with understanding the power that animates their body. The incredible, invisible power that beats your heart, gives you your breath and blood flow may be a start to understanding that you are larger than just your physical self. Whatever you wish your spiritual connection to become, paste onto these pages here.

CHAPTER TWO:
FOCUSING ON PHYSICAL AUTHENTICITY

When I say, "Be authentic!" many people will assume this means in their personality, the way they interact with others, and how they engage in their professional and personal lives. But authenticity is more than just how others perceive you – it's the physical manifestation of the *real you*.

Have you ever looked in the mirror and thought, "I never thought I'd be this overweight," or "What I look like isn't what I feel inside"? So many of us, especially in the U.S., are overloaded by images of what we *should* look like and we are stuck feeling horrible about the exterior that others see. What is less authentic than looking like someone you're not – or worse – someone you don't *desire* to be?

In this section, we're going to dive in to all the ways you can change your body and how you feel about your body *today*. Most of us believe that the right diet or the right pair of jeans will make us feel better about ourselves and make us look amazing. But the truth is that feeling like we possess a body that reflects our inner emotions and personality is more important than looking like what society says you should.

Physical authenticity is twofold: how you take care of yourself and what you surround yourself with. We're going to break this section into what you can do for your body to make it the healthiest reflection of YOU, as well as what you can change about your physical world to become truly authentic.

Take the steps in this section to help you develop your most authentic body.

2.1 Personal Health

As you are probably well aware, there are thousands of studies and research findings that indicate the power of exercise, diet, and general attention to our health increases our happiness, improves our energy, decreases our risk of disease, and helps us engage in more positive relationships and work.

So, let me ask you: Are you being authentic in your personal health? Or do you stress eat, avoid working out, or just *love* junk food? While all of us are guilty of these things from time-to-time, soon you'll wake up and think, "How did I get here?" This, my friend, is the true definition of being unauthentic.

I hope you take the Personal Health Tips in this section seriously, and really start revamping your body from the inside out. Once you do, you'll not only shed pounds and inches, but you'll shed the need to doubt yourself, loathe yourself, and let what others (and society) think affect you.

MY NEW SELF-STYLE

IN-VISION BOARD
CUT & PASTE PAGE

Look through magazines or get images from the internet that depict how you would like your new self-style to be. How do you see the new you? Are you more conservative in your look or are you looking for a more "free" style? Think about your weekly dress, weekend look, and special occasions. Are you a city slicker or more of a country cowboy/girl? Or is a sophisticated and classy look appealing to you? Relaxed fit? How do you present yourself to the world and how do you present yourself when you are alone during self-reflection time? Are they the same or very different? Be free to explore and set your new style.

> **Personal Health Tip #1:**
> **Become a chiropractic patient and do a 6-month program of spinal rehabilitation.**

Chiropractic dates far back as Ancient Greece and is mentioned in the works of mathematicians, scientists, and philosophers. Hippocrates, the "father of medicine," made it his mission to find out what caused disease in humans. At the time, Hippocrates did not believe in viewing disease as restricted to a single area of the body, but rather knew it needed a 'holistic' (whole) methodology that could attack the cause, not just the symptoms. Hippocrates' later works mention chiropractic care, particularly with respect to spinal manipulation's restorative power. Chiropractic care is rooted in ancient medical practices, despite the ignorance of the public today.

Chiropractic care is highly overlooked by most people seeking healthcare for a variety of reasons: high blood pressure, stomach and gastric issues, joint pain, migraines, and even bigger, more serious diseases. But these can all be improved when the spine is finally able to fully communicate with the body, and the body with the brain. Your spine is the body's prime messenger system; help it get the messages across! If the flow is inhibited, so are the instructions the brain sends to the organs and body parts involved!

For so much more on this topic, and how to heal naturally, read BE A MASTER® OF MAXIMUM HEALING in the BE A MASTER® series. www.BEAMASTER.com

Will do ☐ on date: _____ Completed ☐ on _____

Reflect on how this changed or improved your life:
_____

Friends you can invite to do this activity with:
_____

> **Personal Health Tip #2:**
> **Get a massage every other week.**

It's important to get pampered by a Swedish or stone massage, and it's also important to work out the toxins that build up in our muscles. Deep connective tissue manipulation, or 'rolfing', is especially helpful for resetting the muscular system, and also helps in detoxing the lymph and muscular systems. This type of therapy is especially relevant if you sit at a desk all day. Research this and other deep massage techniques; indulge in health and relaxation!

You can also read more on loving yourself in my book, BE A MASTER® OF SELF LOVE.

Will do ☐ on date: _____ Completed ☐ on _____

Reflect on how this changed or improved your life:
_____

Friends you can invite to do this activity with:
_____

Personal Health Tip #3:
Start taking cold showers every morning.

It's not as miserable as it sounds; it actually rejuvenates your skin, scalp, and blood vessels. This helps your circulation and removes the need to 'wake up' using caffeine. Plus you won't waste excess water! A Win-Win-Win situation!

Will do ☐ on date: _____ Completed ☐ on _____

Reflect on how this changed or improved your life:
_____

Personal Health Tip #4:
Switch from commercial coffees to Greek coffee.

Greek coffee gives fewer caffeine 'jitters' and has more polyphenols and antioxidants than the regular beans you normally buy. All of that combines to actually improve heart health and nutritional balance, while also preventing you from a caffeine addiction. Studies show use of this coffee may actually prolong life, as seen in 'blue zones' across the world like Ikaria, Greece.

Will do ☐ on date: _____ Completed ☐ on _____

Reflect on how this changed or improved your life:
_____

Friends you can invite to do this activity with:
_____

> ### Personal Health Tip #5:
> ### Stop eating sugar in junk foods, drinks, and snacks.

That probably seems like a tall order, but I promise you this will change your life! Sugar actually has the same effects as cocaine on the brain, triggering dopamine receptors. That's why you're so crabby when you crave sugary sweet foods or drinks; you're in withdrawal!

Removing excess and unnatural sugars from your diet will not only help you lose weight, but will keep your organs operating efficiently, reduce cavities, improve sleep, and keep you feeling fuller longer. You'll also be less likely to develop diseases like diabetes as you age.

If you're worried about cutting out all sugars from your diet, start small. Cut out sodas immediately and drink tea or natural juice to get that "sugar fix." Once you've acclimated, try cutting out junk food bit by bit.

Will do ☐ on date: _____ Completed ☐ on _____

Reflect on how this changed or improved your life:
_____

> **Personal Health Tip #6:**
>
> **Hire a personal trainer to keep you accountable.**

A personal trainer is *trained* to get you in shape. Not only that, but you can benefit from the camaraderie of working with a professional. Their expertise will be unmatched and you'll have personalized boxing or training workouts designed for you that are effective. Most of all, though, your trainer will make sure you show up. You can read more on this topic and how to lose weight naturally in **BE A MASTER® OF SELF IMAGE**.

Will do ☐ on date: _____ Completed ☐ on _____

Reflect on how this changed or improved your life:
_____

Friends you can invite to do this activity with:
_____

List some ideas on how you can improve on your health and wellness:
_____
_____
_____
_____
_____
_____
_____
_____
_____
_____
_____
_____
_____

MY NEW BODY

IN-VISION BOARD
CUT & PASTE PAGE

∼∼∼

Look through magazines or get images from the internet that depict how you would like your new body to look. How do you see your body in the NEW mirror? Not the current you, the NEW healthier, stronger, leaner you! What is the body you desire? You may have photos of yourself professionally Photo-shopped and then put on the page as inspiration for the new body you will develop, or find photos in fitness magazines that realistically represent you and your body type at its best possible fitness level! You can add photos in the gym, working out with a friend, or whatever reminds you of your fun fitness goals. You can even remove the current face and paste <u>your face from another photo</u> on top of the body of the image! This page is all about you and your new bod. SEE yourself as the new you; let your imagination fly and go for that which you desire!

∼∼∼

> ### Personal Health Tip #7:
> ### Be hypnotized for self-improvement.

Hypnotism is not what most people think it is; it is the art of circumventing the conscious mind to get to what is *really* in the deep subconscious mind. There are a number of benefits to hypnotism, including: breaking bad habits, understanding traumas, overcoming stress or anxious reactions, helping with sleep, and solving problems that seem too difficult to heal using conventional methods. Regression hypnotherapy is particularly useful in deep self-discovery as mentioned in **BE A MASTER® OF PSYCHIC ENERGY.**

Find a licensed, experienced hypnotist in your area and just try it!

Will do ☐ on date: _____ Completed ☐ on _____

Reflect on how this changed or improved your life:
_____

Friends you can invite to do this activity with:
_____

> ### Personal Health Tip #8:
> ### Take on a new sport.

One of the things many people are guilty of is falling into the routine of "Same Old, Same Old." This is even more true when we talk about our physical activities; we work out at the gym 3 nights a week, we run 4 miles a day, we do yoga every morning. But what about a little variety? Did you know that trying a new physical activity produces new connections in the brain that can actually keep your brain (and body) healthy as you age?

Not only that, but new exercise and sports can keep your joints, bones, and cardiovascular system in tip top shape. Browse through your local recreation center's sports teams or get online. Whatever you do, make sure it's new and fun!

Will do ☐ on date: _____ Completed ☐ on _____

Reflect on how this changed or improved your life:
_____

Friends you can invite to do this activity with:
_____

Personal Health Tip #9:

Go for a bike ride.

When is the last time you rode your bike just for fun? Bikes can improve our joint and cardiovascular health, as well as help us lose that pesky belly fat that loves to stick around. But more than anything, it gets you outside in the fresh air, away from the computer or TV, and gets you focused on your body and the world around you.

Will do ☐ on date: _____ Completed ☐ on _____

Reflect on how this changed or improved your life:
_____

Friends you can invite to do this activity with:
_____

Personal Health Tip #10:

Find a fancy new recipe for dinner and invite over family and/or friends.

Try a new dish with salmon (high in Omega3 fatty acids), fresh vegetables, and minimal oils or sauces. Keep your food fresh and light. Oh, and don't forget the red wine!

Will do ☐ on date: _____ Completed ☐ on _____

Reflect on how this changed or improved your life:
_____

Friends you can invite to do this activity with:
_____

> ### Personal Health Tip #11:
> ### Try pranayama breathing.

This is also known as alternate nostril breathing. This is a common yoga practice but can also be introduced into your meditation sessions. Focus on holding one nostril closed while you breathe deeply in and out of the open one. After a few breaths, alternate.

Will do ☐ on date: _____ Completed ☐ on _____

Reflect on how this changed or improved your life:

_____

> ### Personal Health Tip #12:
> ### Go to the doctor to get a checkup.

While you don't have to agree to all the tests or treatments a doctor may recommend, it's always wise to stay on top of your health and to make sure that things are working well before you fall apart. You can also get some great insights into your genetic makeup, your predispositions to disease, and what can be done for certain problems you've been experiencing.

Will do ☐ on date: _____ Completed ☐ on _____

Reflect on how this changed or improved your life:

_____

Friends you can invite to do this activity with:

_____

> ### Personal Health Tip #13:
> ### Donate blood (if you can).

While not everyone can donate blood due to family history or conditions, you should at least see if you're a candidate. If you can donate, try to donate once every month or two. Natural disasters, tragedies, and just regular use in hospitals make blood one of the consistent needs for the medical field.

This also invokes the Law of Abundance; you are giving *life* to someone else. What better way to be thankful for the abundance of life you have pumping through your veins?

Will do ☐ on date: _____ Completed ☐ on _____

Reflect on how this changed or improved your life:
_____

Friends you can invite to do this activity with:
_____

Personal Health Tip #14:
Eat lunch outside.

If you work in an office, go eat your lunch outside – even if the weather is not ideal. Try to soak up as much fresh air as you can. Appreciate the sun, wind, rain, or snow. Invite your coworker(s) to join you.

Will do ☐ on date: _____ Completed ☐ on _____

Reflect on how this changed or improved your life:
_____

Friends you can invite to do this activity with:
_____

Personal Health Tip #15:
Start tracking your activity levels.

You could get an activity band, write down your exercise, or even do a "Calories Burned" log. Technology and apps make this super easy now. With each day, record how you feel. In no time, you'll be able to see how much better you feel when you are exercising more.

Will do ☐ on date: _____ Completed ☐ on _____

Reflect on how this changed or improved your life:
_____

Friends you can invite to do this activity with:
_____

> ### Personal Health Tip #16:
> **Set your alarm for 1 minute earlier every day.**

Do this until you've built up to a time that allows you to meditate in the morning, enjoy your breakfast, and start your day without rushing. This differs for everyone, but you'll know it when you get to that time; you'll feel rested and get to work or start your day off with a smile.

Will do ☐ on date: _____ Completed ☐ on _____

Reflect on how this changed or improved your life:
_____

> ### Personal Health Tip #17:
> **Use a Pomodoro timer on your desktop or phone if you sit at a desk.**

The Pomodoro method is designed to get you working and "in the zone" for 25 minutes. When the timer is up, get up and move around for about 5 minutes and then sit down to another 25 minute session. After 4 sessions, take a longer, 20-30 minute break. Your body and mind will thank you!

Will do ☐ on date: _____ Completed ☐ on _____

Reflect on how this changed or improved your life:
_____

Personal Health Tip #18:
Focus on losing weight in small increments.

Studies show that it takes burning 3,500 calories to lose one pound of fat, so focus on burning that many calories in a week. Keep in mind that the daily caloric intake for most people is 2,000 calories a day. For natural ways to lose weight and get fit see my book **BE A MASTER®OF SELF-IMAGE. www.BEAMASTER.com**

Will do ☐ on date: _____ Completed ☐ on _____

Reflect on how this changed or improved your life:
_____

Personal Health Tip #19:
Drink water instead of over-eating.

Whenever you think you are hungry, try drinking a full glass of water instead. Your body can send mixed signals to your brain which means most of us overeat when we are simply thirsty.

Will do ☐ on date: _____ Completed ☐ on _____

Reflect on how this changed or improved your life:
_____

Personal Health Tip #20:
Meal plan for the week.

Focus on eating mostly green, nutrient-rich vegetables and healthy fats. The less processed sugar, wheat, and carbohydrates you put in your meals, the better you will feel and the less foggy your mind will be.

For more information on what you should plan to eat, read BE A MASTER® OF MAXIMUM HEALING. www.BEAMASTER.com

Will do ☐ on date: _____ Completed ☐ on _____

Reflect on how this changed or improved your life:

_____

Personal Health Tip #21:

Try for 10,000 steps every day.

Whether walking to and from your car, around your office, or going for a long walk, try to get in 10,000 steps a day. You can get a small pedometer, treat yourself to a nice activity tracker band, Or use an app on your phone. It's a great idea to get coworkers, friends, or relatives involved to make it a friendly competition.

Will do ☐ on date: _____ Completed ☐ on _____

Reflect on how this changed or improved your life:

_____

Friends you can invite to do this activity with:

_____

Personal Health Tip #22:

Cut back on any drinks that are not water.

Sodas and sugary juices can make our bodies acidic, which leads to dis-ease. Cutting down on caffeinated drinks and alcoholic beverages will help our bodies stay in prime condition. Sugar and caffeine act like cocaine in our systems, activating the pleasure and reward centers of our brain.

This is why we crave those drinks so much more than water, and why we get so cranky when we can't have them. If you're drinking something that sends you through withdrawals, it's time to cut it out!

Will do ☐ on date: _____ Completed ☐ on _____

Reflect on how this changed or improved your life:

_____

Friends you can invite to do this activity with:
_____

Personal Health Tip #23:

Try "power naps."

Most people don't nap because they know they'll either a.) oversleep b.) feel less rested when they wake up. But studies have shown that there is a science to the "power nap." Try taking a little snooze in the afternoon if you have a workplace or schedule that allows for it. Stick to only 10-20 minutes and see how energized you feel when it's all over.

The key to this, though, is making sure you sleep well at night. Commit to 7-8 hours a night, listening to your body's natural rhythm when it says it asks to sleep or be awake!

Will do ☐ on date: _____ Completed ☐ on _____

Reflect on how this changed or improved your life:
_____

Personal Health Tip #24:

Always pack 2-3 healthy snacks.

Especially if you work away from home all day, you should always have a healthy snack with you. This way, you keep your metabolism in a healthy place and you avoid impulse buys and impulse eats. You can also feel great about having a nice, healthy, light snack in your bag just in case!

Will do ☐ on date: _____ Completed ☐ on _____

Reflect on how this changed or improved your life:
_____

> **Personal Health Tip #25:**
> **Buy the majority of your produce from organic sources.**

There are numerous studies out there that show the risks of eating "conventional" produce. There are heavy metals, toxins, pesticides, fungicides, and even *lye* on some produce. Most nutritionists, dieticians, and food experts recommend that you eat as much organic food as possible to avoid these nasty additions.

If you're worried about the cost of or access to organic food, I recommend focusing on these: Peaches, Apples, Celery, Nectarines, Cherries, Pears, Grapes, Spinach, Lettuce, and Potatoes.

For more information on the power of organic food and the risks of conventionally-grown produce, read BE A MASTER® OF MAXIMUM HEALING.

Will do ☐ on date: _____ Completed ☐ on _____

Reflect on how this changed or improved your life:
_____

Friends you can invite to do this activity with:
_____

> **Personal Health Tip #26:**
> **Once a month, watch the sun rise.**

Commit to getting up before the sun and taking a walk somewhere you can see the sun rise. Go alone or take a loved one, but focus on not talking or distracting yourself with music, phones, etc. Just take in the beauty of nature and relish the quiet.

This not only gets your blood pumping early (to help you have a very productive day), but it also gets you in your body and out in nature – two very powerful tools for developing your most authentic body!

Will do ☐ on date: _____ Completed ☐ on _____

Reflect on how this changed or improved your life:
_____

Friends you can invite to do this activity with:

_____

> **Personal Health Tip #27:**
>
> **Take a dance class.**

Whether you're a man or woman, you can benefit from a nice, fun dance class. There are tons of dance styles, from salsa and tango to ballet or hip-hop. This is a very active, challenging exercise but it's also just plain fun.

Will do ☐ on date: _____ Completed ☐ on _____

Reflect on how this changed or improved your life:

_____

Friends you can invite to do this activity with:

_____

> **Personal Health Tip #28:**
>
> **Bake a healthier version of your favorite dessert.**

As you've probably started cutting out your sugar intake thanks to the previous challenges, it's time to reward yourself!

Whether brownies, cookies, or cake, find your favorite dessert in a healthier recipe version. There are tons of vegan, sugar-free, wheat-free options that taste amazing! You can have your cake and eat it too – guilt-free!

Will do ☐ on date: _____ Completed ☐ on _____

Reflect on how this changed or improved your life:

_____

Friends you can invite to do this activity with:

_____

> ### Personal Health Tip #29:
> ### Replace cow's milk with almond, hemp, or coconut milk.

The antibiotics, hormones, and general yuck found in conventional milk is not safe for you. Choose a plant-based alternative with fewer sugars, less fat, and fewer chemicals and fillers. You can also use these alternative milk options for baking and cooking, so you don't have to worry about that!

For more on this, read BE A MASTER® OF MAXIMUM HEALING. www.BEA-MASTER.com

Will do ☐ on date: _____ Completed ☐ on _____

Reflect on how this changed or improved your life:

_____

> ### Personal Health Tip #30:
> ### Visit a certified holistic nutritionist.

Not only can these specialists give you some great recipes and options for finding food that is healthy and delicious, but they can also evaluate *your* specific dietary needs. A lot of us don't know that our bodies all have certain quirks, vitamin deficiencies, and metabolisms, so most diets don't work.

When you visit a holistic nutritionist, they will be able to evaluate your current food intake and decide what's working and what's not. They can also test for deficiencies, allergies, and sensitivities!

From there, you can cut out what doesn't sit well with your body and eat more of what your body loves: leafy greens, healthy fats, and fresh food!

Will do ☐ on date: _____ Completed ☐ on _____

Reflect on how this changed or improved your life:

_____

Personal Health Tip #31:
Try a short, 10-minute yoga video on YouTube.

Next time you're just sitting on the couch, binging on videos, sit down on the floor and do a session of yoga. Yoga straightens the spine, strengthens and tones your muscle, and powers your chakras. While you may not feel like you've just worked out, your energy and body will feel different.

For more information on your chakras and spinal stretches, check out BE A MASTER® OF PSYCHIC ENERGY. www.BEAMASTER.com

Will do ☐ on date: _____ Completed ☐ on _____

Reflect on how this changed or improved your life:
_____

Friends you can invite to do this activity with:
_____

Personal Health Tip #32:
Leave at least 4 bites of food on your plate.

Just because you dished out a large serving doesn't mean you have to eat it! If you feel guilty about it, save the leftovers or let someone else eat it. Our stomachs learn to expect a large amount of food and stretch accordingly; it's time to shrink it back down!

Will do ☐ on date: _____ Completed ☐ on _____

Reflect on how this changed or improved your life:
_____

Personal Health Tip #33:
Stand up straight.

No, I'm not your mother, but I will say it again: Stand up straight! Your posture is *powerful.* Not only does it strengthen your spine, but it also projects an energy of confidence and sexuality. It's simple but so effective!

For more on this and other tips about projecting confidence, read BE A MASTER® OF SELF IMAGE. www.BEAMASTER.com

Will do ☐ on date: _____ Completed ☐ on _____

Reflect on how this changed or improved your life:
_____

Personal Health Tip #34:
Have an aura image taken.

Have your aura photo taken. There are many places online that offer this service. You will learn a lot about your energy field and how your emotions and thoughts may affect your current state of being. Search online for "Dr. Theo Kousouli Aura Imaging" for the videos or visit my website at www.drkousouli.com for more information on the aura. I explain, in much detail, the aspects of auras and their meaning in my book **BE A MASTER® OF PSYCHIC ENERGY. www.BEAMASTER.com.**

Will do ☐ on date: _____ Completed ☐ on _____

Reflect on how this changed or improved your life:
_____

Friends you can invite to do this activity with:
_____

Personal Health Tip #35:
Buy a Himalayan salt lamp.

If you can, buy a Himalayan salt lamp and place it in your home where you spend the most time. These lamps are made from some amazing chunks of salt that may release healing ions into the air. This can help if you suffer from asthma or allergies and can increase energy levels. Plus they're just really beautiful to look at and your pet will definitely be drawn to it!

Will do ☐ on date: _____ Completed ☐ on _____

Reflect on how this changed or improved your life:
_____

Personal Health Tip #36:
Make lemonade - or any juice - from scratch.

Buy the fruit, prep it, squeeze it, mix it, and chill it. Don't add extra sugars, but you can add other fruit juices for flavor. You can even freeze these for ice cubes on a hot summer day, or make popsicles! Healthy, fun, cheap, and tasty!

This will help with those pesky sugar cravings, as well as get you an all-natural dose of fruit; it's a win-win!

Will do ☐ on date: _____ Completed ☐ on _____

Reflect on how this changed or improved your life:
_____

Friends you can invite to do this activity with:
_____

Personal Health Tip #37:
Invite your friends for a barbeque or cookout.

This is where you can show off your newly-found healthy cooking abilities. Grill salmon and fresh veggies over the fire (but not for too long). Have a nice, fresh salad and maybe some of that juice you just squeezed. The benefits of this are threefold: 1. You get to eat some delicious, healthy food. 2. Your friends get to eat delicious, healthy food. 3. You're outside, enjoying yourselves!

Don't underestimate the power of a group meal. There is a reason that this is so common in France and Italy; social eating is a way of life. You eat less, have more laughs, and eat quality food made with love.

Will do ☐ on date: _____ Completed ☐ on _____

Reflect on how this changed or improved your life:
_____

Friends you can invite to do this activity with:
_____

> **Personal Health Tip #38:**
>
> **Get a sleep study done.**

Sleep is one of the biggest areas where most Americans are slacking. We tell ourselves that we don't need much sleep or "there are more important things," but the truth is that sleep is one of the best ways to prevent dis-ease. Without sleep, our brains and bodies can't recuperate. Many CEOs and famous people will also admit to cherishing their sleep, and consider it just as important as their nutrition and exercise.

If you are experiencing sleep apnea, extreme fatigue, or problems staying asleep, ask your doctor to send you in for a professional sleep study. These overnight studies can supply you with a wealth of information as you sleep in their lab while monitored. You should, however, also perform your own mini-sleep study for your own self-awareness and self-discovery.

To know if your sleep cycle and schedule are working for you or against you, purchase and set up a video camera that has night vision or low light filming capability. Go to bed, allowing the camera to record all through the night. Review the footage in the morning in both fast-forward and normal speed. Look at the recorded timer for how long it took you to fall asleep, how many hours you slept, how deep your breathing was, how much you tossed and turned, if you snored, if you maintained your sleeping position, if you dreamt (will require you to videotape closer to your face while monitoring for rapid eyelid movement), if you talked in your sleep, or if you sleepwalked.

Do this overnight for a week and adapt your sleep habits and schedules around your findings. If you feel your sleep patterns are abnormal, you should discuss this with your doctor and share your findings with them.

Will do ☐ on date: _____ Completed ☐ on _____

Reflect on how this changed or improved your life:
_____

Personal notes for more self improvement:

_____
_____
_____
_____
_____
_____
_____
_____
_____
_____
_____
_____
_____
_____
_____
_____
_____
_____
_____
_____
_____
_____
_____

CHAPTER THREE:
Clearing Our Mental Space to Make Way for Authenticity

When you were introduced to the concept of the "authentic self" in the introduction, odds are you thought of how you interact with yourself *internally*. Our minds are our most powerful tools; we can use them to shape our reality and even change it. Many of us are also concerned that our minds are too "unruly" or "unreliable" when it comes to developing our true selves and establishing new behaviors, habits, and lifestyles.

And so we let ourselves get tricked into following the crowd, buying into the latest fad, and believing like everyone else believes. It also leads us to never question our own behaviors, habits, or lifestyle. How many times have you said, "It's just what people do!" or "I don't have any control over that"? Before my own personal revolution, I felt very much the victim, very much a product of my circumstances.

It wasn't until I really started to realize that the way I was *feeling* about what I was *thinking* was creating the world I lived in. In my time since this revelation, and since my growth both personally and professionally, I have come to realize that what I think and where I put my mental energy are the core of who I am. So why would I desire someone (or something) else to shape my reality?

Because our mind is in control of our current and future circumstances, I desire to address the need for clearing our personal mental space and also projecting a mental image for what we desire to physically manifest. The first part of this section will show you how to clear that mental space and get to the root of who you are "in your head," so that you can then take the tips from the second half of this section to manifest your best and most authentic reality.

I'm going to show you just how capable your mind is at shaping your reality and changing YOU and your life for the better. You'll get a ton of usable, bite-sized tips to help you change your inner monologue from "I can't" to "I absolutely can… and I am!"

3.1 Creating Mental Space

Authenticity starts with how we talk to ourselves. It stems from our ability to "be at home" in our own heads. How often can you just be alone with your thoughts? How often do you distract yourself or call a friend over because you just can't be alone? Or worse yet, how often do you avoid change or things that shake you up because you are stuck in your ways?

This is the root of the authenticity problem: We don't desire to expand our horizons because that requires evaluating our current state of being and thinking. This section might prove to be uncomfortable for some of us, especially those who avoid taking a look under the hood.

I compel you to take these Personal Space Tips to heart; try them, use them daily if you can. And most of all, take note of how these tips and tasks help you clear that personal mental space to make room for new thoughts, new behaviors, and the best YOU possible.

> **Creating Mental Space Tip #1:**
> **Take up meditation and meditate daily.**

Meditation is a lifelong practice, one that you never truly "master." Many people let this discourage them from ever trying, without understanding the real benefits to a short, simple daily practice.

To start your meditation practice, simply review your daily events in your mind before you go to bed and wake up envisioning your day in a positive manner. Lay out the events you wish to experience. There are also a number of other ways to meditate, but there is no *wrong* way.

If you'd like to really delve deeply into this, check out BE A MASTER® OF PSYCHIC ENERGY available at www.BEAMASTER.com.

Will do ☐ on date: _____ Completed ☐ on _____

Reflect on how this changed or improved your life:
_____

Friends you can invite to do this activity with:
_____

> **Creating Mental Space Tip #2:**
> **Learn to Lucid dream.**

Over my years of practice, I noticed that a lot of my patients were not doing well with sleep. I knew that if I could help them maximize their REM cycles and help them control their dreams, they would be better off both during sleep and also during their awake state. I developed my version of lucid dreaming, called KLDT™, which I teach in my seminars.

The benefits of **Kousouli® Lucid Dream Technique** are many. When you balance out and optimize your sleep cycles, along with the sympathetic and parasympathetic functions of the autonomic system, you can experience deeper relaxation, rapid rejuvenation, more creativity, excellent moods, and you will fall asleep faster.

Many of my patients claim to feel a huge boost in confidence and self-esteem while lowering their performance anxiety in sports, at work, or in school. They are able to have more memorable, pleasant yet intense sleep states that yield positive effects for a more productive life while awake. They can even materialize the guidance they received in their dream state and apply it during their awake state. Lucid dreaming also speeds up healing and may be able to stop or reverse possible disease processes in their tracks by auto-repair of body systems.

How to lucid dream

A lucid dream is a vivid dream you are aware of and can control. You will be aware you are dreaming, but you won't fully wake up. You can actively control your dreams and manipulate them. To have a lucid dream, before going to bed each night, tell yourself you will have a lucid dream and that you will be able to remember it. Keep a dream journal by your bed so that you can write immediately once you wake up every morning. Keep track of reoccurring themes and note the most memorable items, as those will have meaning to them later (which you will research through dream dictionaries online).

When you wake up every morning, lay still for a moment and recall the dream's details. You must immediately record them or you will forget them. Taking vitamin B6, melatonin, SAM-e, Choline Bitartrate and 5-HTP may improve the dream cycle. Over time you will learn to take control of the dreams and have them more often. How long varies on many factors, including your sleep cycle and hours of sleep per night. Children usually can have lucid dreams easily, as they can let go of worries and fears and allow themselves a lighter playful existence.

Persons with heavy worrisome psyches usually have nightmares and scary dreams, as they carry much of their worries into the rest state. Learning to lucid dream will help you confront your subconscious issues and gain access to invaluable information from the other side of the veil. Many of my patients who have learned how to lucid dream using **KLDT**™ have brought back information, like a new piece of music, art, or solutions to personal problems.

Will do ☐ on date: _____ Completed ☐ on _____

Reflect on how this changed or improved your life:
_____

Journal your dream experiences here IMMEDIATELY UPON AWAKING:

MY DREAM STATE

IN-VISION BOARD
CUT & PASTE PAGE

Look through magazines or get images from the internet that depict your most beautiful dream state. You are free to create as your heart desires. Create a dream you wish to dream or take part in. Allow your imagination to run wild and put the aspects of the dream you wish to have in a collage on this page. The important thing in this exercise is to allow your imagination an open window to create.

> **Creating Mental Space Tip #3:**
>
> Purge your home.

Many of us accrue tons of stuff in our homes, from impulse buys to gifts from the parents. Instead of removing junk as it comes in, though, we tend to just "organize it" or put it somewhere we don't have to see it. Not only does this lead to a cluttered physical space, but it has a massive impact on our mental space.

Take small steps each day to remove all the bad energy clutter. There are tons of resources online, but I recommend that you remove 1 thing each day that doesn't bring you joy or serve a purpose. Soon, you'll start getting rid of stuff just because it feels good and you know you don't need it!

You can also read more on this topic in BE A MASTER® OF PSYCHIC ENERGY.

Will do ☐ on date: _____ Completed ☐ on _____

Reflect on how this changed or improved your life:
_____

Family members you can invite to do this activity with:
_____

List items you wish to donate to others:
_____
_____
_____
_____
_____
_____
_____
_____
_____
_____

MY PERSONAL HOME SPACE

IN-VISION BOARD
CUT & PASTE PAGE

❧❧❧

Look through magazines or get images from the internet that depict the perfect home and what that looks like to you. Imagine you just purchased it and are going to decorate the yard, the fence, the interior. Everything! As you paste the photos and pictures that look like your new home, how does it feel to live in this home? What does this home provide your soul and what does it mean for you to live here? What would your neighbors be like, and what does the community look like? What country is this home (or homes) in? Let your imagination run wild - there are no wrong answers here!

❧❧❧

> **Creating Mental Space Tip #4:**
> **One in, one out.**

For every one item you bring into your home besides food, make sure to send one thing out. We all have more than we need. This helps you develop a strong mental awareness of what you have in your home, what you *need*, and how many other people in the world aren't as lucky as you are.

Developing your authentic self by focusing on what you allow into your home will strengthen your authentic mind, as well.

Will do ☐ on date: _____ Completed ☐ on _____

Reflect on how this changed or improved your life:
_____

Family members you can invite to do this activity with:
_____

> **Creating Mental Space Tip #5:**
> **Watch a documentary.**

Try watching a documentary about the environment, nature, a specific argument / lifestyle, or a phenomenon you don't know about. You can rent these on Netflix or rent physical copies from your local library.

Learn something new and think about what you can do to make the world a better place in your own way.

Will do ☐ on date: _____ Completed ☐ on _____

Reflect on how this changed or improved your life:
_____

Friends you can invite to do this activity with:
_____

Creating Mental Space Tip #6:
Disagree with yourself.

Watch a documentary or read a book about a perspective, law, or person that you firmly disagree with. For example, if you're a diehard Liberal, try reading a book about conservative policies. If you're strictly about Western medicine, watch documentaries about how many people use Eastern or alternative medicines.

Expand your mind and maybe change your position! Life is all about growth, and authenticity can't be found until you know where you stand in the world!

Will do ☐ on date: _____ Completed ☐ on _____

Reflect on how this changed or improved your life:
_____

Friends you can invite to do this activity with:
_____

Creating Mental Space Tip #7:
Start creating.

Start making your own art, whether it is photography (see the world in a new way), painting, sketching, or even sculpting. You can take up knitting, start playing with your sewing machine, or make up a skit. Whatever makes you feel great and gets your brain making new connections – that's what you should be doing.

The benefits of having an artistic hobby include: improved happiness, decreased rates of dementia as you age, increased mental acuity, improved problem-solving skills, and – of course – cool art!

Will do ☐ on date: _____ Completed ☐ on _____

Reflect on how this changed or improved your life:
_____

Friends you can invite to do this activity with:
_____

> **Creating Mental Space Tip #8:**
> **Start journaling.**

For some, this may just look like a small notebook to jot down thoughts, but for others it could be a bullet journal, a diary of sorts, or even an art journal full of paint or colors. Get creative and get your thoughts on paper; they're much easier to organize once they're written down.

You'll notice that your journal will soon become a place where you can "leave it all on the table" so that you step away feeling refreshed and lighter. While we all have stresses and problems in our lives, we don't have to let them bog us down and keep our mental space occupied. Your journal can serve as the place where you store those non-serving thoughts to make room for the thoughts that help you grow as an authentic person.

Will do ☐ on date: _____ Completed ☐ on _____

Reflect on how this changed or improved your life:

_____

> **Creating Mental Space Tip #9:**
> **Keep a small pocket notebook with you at all times.**

Sort of like journaling, but less personal, keep a small notebook with you when you go out. This is so that you can write down great thoughts, save business cards, or write down those lists you always forget before you get home. This is a great way to keep track of your progress and to connect with your Mastermind groups. If you don't know what a Mastermind group is or how it can help you, check out **BE A MASTER® OF SUCCESS**. www.BEAMASTER.com.

Will do ☐ on date: _____ Completed ☐ on _____

Reflect on how this changed or improved your life:

_____

> **Creating Mental Space Tip #10:**
> **Read a biography of someone you admire.**

What famous figures do you admire, like Albert Einstein or Oprah? Pick up their biography or autobiography and learn from their life story. While we often assume that these people are just flukes, people who "got lucky," that is often very far from the truth.

Not only will this expand your literary tastes, but you always have something new to learn. You'll also be able to clarify your own problems and how to get from Point A to Point Z, just like your idols did.

Will do ☐ on date: _____ Completed ☐ on _____

Reflect on how this changed or improved your life:
_____

If you had a board of representatives who advised and counseled you, who would they be?

_____
_____
_____
_____
_____
_____
_____
_____
_____
_____
_____
_____
_____

PEOPLE I ADMIRE

IN-VISION BOARD
CUT & PASTE PAGE

◈◈◈

Look through magazines or get images from the internet and find the people you highly admire as real, authentic role models throughout history, both past and presently living. Was it Jesus? Inventors like Nikola Tesla or the Wright brothers? Perhaps it's a President of the United States or political figure like Winston Churchill? Maybe a truly famous inspirational musician or artist like Michael Jackson or actor like Al Pacino? If you were to ask anyone for advice in life or have them in your "inner" circle, who would it be? Surround your page with all people you find inspirational and motivate you to be a better person. Be sure to look into their history and what made them great; don't simply put a figure on the board for fame - choose ones that made a difference in the world and were authentic. Not all famous people deserve to be real role models.

◈◈◈

> **Creating Mental Space Tip #11:**
> **Go to a poetry or literary reading.**

If you desire to truly know yourself and what your tastes are, you have to try on a lot of different hats, so to speak. What better way to learn about yourself and the world around you than to see how others view it?

Pick a close friend who would enjoy a poetry or literary reading, and find a good time at your local café, bookstore, or library. Some art galleries and local boutiques offer artistic experiences like this, as well. Not only will you get to experience spoken art and support local artists, but you'll also get your own mental and creative juices flowing. When we consume the art of others, our brains naturally desire to create art of their own!

Will do ☐ on date: _____ Completed ☐ on _____

Reflect on how this changed or improved your life:
_____

Friends you can invite to do this activity with:
_____

3.2 Mental Manifestation

In my other books, **BE A MASTER® OF PSYCHIC ENERGY** and **BE A MASTER® OF SUCCESS**, I talk in depth about the true power of harnessing our mental energy. Just as you are using the blank pages in this book as your In-Vision board, there is immense power in your thoughts and where your mental energy is spent. Have you ever thought, "Man, I hope I don't get sick!" only to fall ill a day later? Or have you ever thought, "I nailed that interview! I got the job for sure!" to then get a phone call letting you know that you did, in fact, get the job?

It's amazing, the simple power of thought. While just thinking about winning the lottery may not land you in the billionaire category on Forbes, truly harnessing the power of the Law of Attraction and the Law of Abundance will help you raise your energetic vibrations – the level of energy that you put out into the world – so that you can then accept vibrations from higher sources.

What does this mean for your mental authenticity? Think about what would happen if you got to the root of what you TRULY desired; if you got to the root of how you TRULY felt about the world around you. What then? What could you manifest if you had a clear shot at who you truly desired to be?

The tips in this section are going to give you little tasks you can do each day to help build your Mental Manifestation Muscles, as I like to call them. Do these when you can and stick to them. Soon, you'll be a Manifesting Machine.

Mental Manifestation Tip #1:

Go shopping, but not for yourself.

You could buy a nice gift for someone you've been thinking about or you can take a family in need grocery shopping. This will teach you to be grateful to have "extra" money and also attract the Law of Abundance to you. Read more about this in **BE A MASTER® OF PSYCHIC ENERGY. www.BEAMASTER.com**.

Will do ☐ on date: _____ Completed ☐ on _____

Reflect on how this changed or improved your life:
_____

Friends you can invite to do this activity with:
_____

Mental Manifestation Tip #2:

Stop complaining.

Next time you go off about that annoying coworker, talk badly about the service you received at a restaurant, or say something negative about the course of your day, take a minute. The words you speak become your reality, so instead of saying, "Today was horrible," let that thought pass and speak the next positive thing that comes to your mind. You can create a habit and create a happier world in the process.

Will do ☐ on date: _____ Completed ☐ on _____

Reflect on how this changed or improved your life:
_____

> ### Mental Manifestation Tip #3:
> ### Visualize yourself winning.

Try to visualize yourself already possessing something you desire or achieving a goal you have set. You can do this when you're sitting at your desk, riding the bus to work, or instead of watching TV. When we visualize, our mind makes connections that make the brain believe we already have what we desire, and then we attract just that.

You can add your visualization to your In-Vision board at the end of this section, or create a larger In-Vision board to keep up at home.

You can also read more about visualization in BE A MASTER® OF PSYCHIC ENERGY. This is an in-depth, powerful tool that I discuss at length; don't miss out!

Will do ☐ on date: _____ Completed ☐ on _____

Reflect on how this changed or improved your life:

_____

> ### Mental Manifestation Tip #4:
> ### Tell the people who inspire you that they mean a lot to you.

While this may seem like just a little bit of a connection or relationship boost, it's very powerful in terms of universal energy. After all, we all have a creator who has helped us become the people we are today. But we have mentors and other teachers along the way who mold us, shape us, and rattle us to our cores.

Without acknowledging that sort of impact, you're denying the Universe its credit for helping you get where you are. Don't make the mistake of ignoring this; shake the hands that have helped you up.

Let your teachers, mentors, and parents – whoever has inspired you and helped you be a better person - know that they have made a difference.

Will do ☐ on date: _____ Completed ☐ on _____

Reflect on how this changed or improved your life:

_____

> **Mental Manifestation Tip #5:**
> **Find an accountability partner.**

Like the personal trainer in the first section, you should find someone who will hold you accountable for your professional, health, or personal development goals. While this is usually a peer or someone you look up to, I don't always recommend choosing close friends. Friends tend to cut each other slack and will often miss out on their accountability tasks to do things together.

Choose your accountability partner wisely, offer to be their accountability partner, and really make sure that you're going to work so you don't let this person down! Putting this level of commitment into your projects or goals is recognized as positive energy; keep it coming!

Check in daily, weekly, or biweekly with your partner and make sure that you have days to celebrate together when you accomplish something.

Will do ☐ on date: _____ Completed ☐ on _____

Reflect on how this changed or improved your life:
_____

Accountability partner you can invite to do this activity with:
_____

> **Mental Manifestation Tip #6:**
> **Create a "No More" list.**

So often, we make lists of things we desire to do, our goals, and what we want. But what we neglect to do is see what things are getting in the way of us manifesting those desires.

For this reason, I think it's important that you make a "No More" list. It's not as harsh as it sounds, but it does draw a definitive line in the sand about what you are and are not going to tolerate in your mental or physical space as you grow on your authentic journey.

A few ideas could include:
- "No more whining."
- "No more cookies for breakfast."
- "No more binge drinking."
- "No more episodic TV marathons when I have things to do."
- "No more arguing over petty things with my significant other."

These are habits that will take time to break, but the idea is to write the list today and move forward with these intentions in mind. After writing it all down, throw it in the trash!

Will do ☐ on date: _____ Completed ☐ on _____

Reflect on how this changed or improved your life:
_____

Friends you can invite to do this activity with:
_____

> **Mental Manifestation Tip #7:**
> **Participate in gratitude challenges on social media.**

One of the first truths you will learn about the Laws of the Universe is that they are drawn to positive energy. Social media is notorious for being the source of negative energy for many people, especially bragging, political bashing, and envying. You may have engaged in this yourself from time-to-time, and that's OK.

But starting today, you're going to only post things that are positive. This can include things that you are thankful for, and make sure to avoid "humble brags." This will make your followers and friends happy and keep social media a positive influence in your life. It will also show the Universe that you are grateful for what you have and are not envious or covetous of others.

Will do ☐ on date: _____ Completed ☐ on _____

Reflect on how this changed or improved your life:
_____

> **Mental Manifestation Tip #8:**
>
> **Write positive affirmations on Post-It Notes.**

The power of the written word should not be underestimated. This is why I've given you a couple of tips about journaling, writing lists, and writing letters. But positive affirmations are different than organizing your mental space; they're designed to make sure that your mental space is positive, healthy, and authentic.

An affirmation can look like anything, but my only rule is that you do not include a negative in your note. This means that you should not write things like, "I am not fat," "I am not stupid," "I have no time for mean people." While those things may seem OK, the Universe sees everything we tell ourselves as true without discriminating against the negatives in the sentence. This means that the Universe hears "fat," "stupid," "mean people," and that's not what you desire to attract!

Instead, write the most positive words in the most positive structure possible. Leave them on your bathroom mirror, on your computer screen, on the fridge. Try:

- I am creative and capable.
- I have a healthy relationship with food.
- I am a source of energy and light.
- I attract abundance.
- I am whole.

Will do ☐ on date: _____ Completed ☐ on _____

Reflect on how this changed or improved your life:

_____

> **Mental Manifestation Tip #9:**
>
> **Get clear on your financial goals.**

I want to be very clear here: Money is a tool. Money does not define you, it does not indicate your self-worth, and it does not serve any other purpose than to give you the life you desire to live. Now, ask yourself: What amount of money do you desire to live the life YOU deserve to live?

If you desire a big house or a nice car, that's part of your mental manifestation. You must attract the job, career, or projects that will give you that amount of money. You must also get clear on other financial goals, like how much you desire to save, what you choose to spend a month on restaurants, and if you *really* need that $300 handbag.

This is one of the biggest aspects of flexing your Mental Manifestation Muscles and taking control of your life. Why? Because our society tells us when, where, and how to spend our money. Taking the time to get really clear on what we actually desire to do with our money (our paper energy, essentially) will remove all those distractions from your mental picture and empower you.

Improve your financial situation: talk to a financial planner about your future or just start sticking to a budget! It's much more exciting than it sounds to be in control of your money. Before you can grow in massive abundance, you must show the Universe that you know how to manage and direct it.

Will do ☐ on date: _____ Completed ☐ on _____

Reflect on how this changed or improved your life:
_____

Debt Elimination Exercise:

I added this section of the book because many people struggle with this and debt has crippled their lives. I have struggled with debt myself and, until I took responsibility to remove it from my life, I was powerless to the mentality of always living to 'catch up' to life. All of this left a huge hole in my joy. Until I learned myself how to manage my financial future, I was unable to feel good about my future, no matter how much I was earning. The simple fact is that you must look at all aspects of your life and balance them to create true authenticity. That means money energy as well.

Unfortunately, our world is financially illiterate and this is orchestrated on purpose to keep the power structure the way it is. However, those who wish to take back their power (like you, since you're reading this!) can and will be able to, simply because they separate themselves from the "old them," previously enslaved to giving their power over to others. Removing your personal debt does wonders for your self-esteem, your buying power, and inner peace.

You cannot ignore debt and let it continue to grow. You must change your perception from being powerless to being powerful. With a change of perception comes a change in attitude and then energy will move toward helping you create abundance. The alternative is staying in and getting deeper into a debt "lack" mentality. Without removing your debt, you remain subservient to your debtors and material possessions that consume you.

Here are some of my favorite quotes about money and debt...

"Today, there are three kinds of people: the have's, the have-not's, and the have-not-paid-for-what-they-have's."
~Earl Wilson

"What can be added to the happiness of a man who is in health, out of debt, and has a clear conscience?"
~Adam Smith

"Debt can turn a free, happy person into a bitter human being."
~Michael Mihalik

"Debt, n. An ingenious substitute for the chain and whip of the slave-driver."
-Ambrose Bierce

"Debt is the worst poverty."
~Thomas Fuller

"A man in debt is so far a slave."
~Ralph Waldo Emerson

So, are you ready to handle that debt?

Take a piece of paper or a notebook and, across the top, write MONTHLY EXPENDITURES. Under that, make a row of all the things you are paying monthly, like: office rent, home mortgage or apartment rent, car payment, groceries, gas, insurance payments, etc. Midpage, write DEBTS FOR ELIMINATION and, under that, make a row of debts you have: school loans, car loans, credit card balances, etc.

On the next page or backside of the paper, write INCOME. Under that line, write all the ways income is coming in. This could be a full-time job, side hustles, child support, or government assistance.

You will soon see the problem with your living habits. You will see in plain numbers how you have overspent and gotten yourself into a financial black hole. But you can get out of it! You just have to funnel your income at the mountains of debt and reverse them back into molehills. Seeing it all written out is so beneficial. No one takes the time to write out a budget and plan to change their circumstances any more. They just charge their credit cards and assume it will always be this way.

Well, no more! You're going to take back your financial responsibility. The biggest piece of this puzzle is being honest with yourself and understanding that you allowed the ease of the credit industry's 'convenience' to overtake your personal financial power. Once you are awake, you can get your power back. Of course, "they" won't like this, but oh well!

You must show the Universe that your vibration of money is changing to demonstrate your ability to flow abundance. Release debt and release your resistance! The Universe will empower you and connect your feelings to your status with money. Nothing is more important than that- your FEELing is your current status with money matters. The vibrational balance of how you feel is huge, especially when it comes to money.

The mantra to memorize and say before you embark on changing your money and debt situation is:

> *"I am willing and able to do all I can to live joyfully and in integrity with my true self, as I take on a humble existence that sustains me while I keep the promise and my word with myself, others I have borrowed from, and other merchants for the goods and services I have purchased, used, and enjoyed. I now acknowledge that I take back my power by putting my monetary focus on eliminating the invisible links of bondage, called debt, so I may enjoy my future sources of income and live a life I am deserving of. I am willing to rough it out for the short term to live better in the long term. I now choose to play the game of debt elimination so that I may experience my total financial power and freedom. With a powerful intention for success and a fun plan of action, I start today and am dedicated to eliminating each column until I am debt free."*

Here are a couple tricks I have for kick starting your authentic financial journey:

o Write down and evaluate your mortgage, credit card balances, doctor's bills, 401(k) loans, personal loans from banks or from family members, student loans, auto loans, home equity loans.

- Attack the highest interest rates first, they are the loans that are growing the fastest. Once you work down the highest interest rate credit cards or loans, you can refocus your financial power into the next largest one and so on, until they are all paid off.

Here are some ideas to help you save money while you are focusing on paying off your debts.

- Do not add more charges to any credit cards, and destroy all credit cards except one or two with the lowest APR%

- Forgo the latte, forgo the meal extras. You really don't need them.

- Focus only on the necessities of life, not the luxuries right now.

- Sell everything taking up space in your home and garage that you don't use. Old clothes, gadgets, gaming consoles, etc. Turn them into cash that goes straight to eliminating your debt faster.

- Refinance your car loan with a credit union to minimize the scale of the loan repayment - they usually have the best rates.

- Reward yourself whenever you eliminate debt. Don't go overboard; choose simple luxuries as a way to celebrate.

- If you can pay down double or triple the minimum payments and revel at the lower statement balance each time you get your statement. Use that as motivation to get it PAID IN FULL!

- Label things as necessity or non-necessity. Necessities are groceries every week or gas for your car. Non-necessities are dining out or buying a new flashy accessory.

- Explain to your friends and family that you are looking to get out of debt and want their loving support to keep you accountable and on point. Don't hang out with people who are not respectful of your debt elimination game.

- Always spend less than you have coming in.

- Entertain yourself in simple ways, visiting friends and family, having a cup of homemade tea or coffee together, spending quality time just being 'present' for each other.

- If you cannot pay for something with cash, don't charge it. You can't afford it.

- Take a bike instead of driving. It saves gas, miles on your car, and gives you great exercise.

- Eat vegetarian. It is very healthy and cheaper than spending money on foods like chicken and beef. You'll save both money and your health.

- Once your debt has been zeroed out, put the money into a savings. Put 65% away and enjoy the remaining 35% on you.

- Keep a sensible budget and plan for emergencies by having an emergency fund.

- Delete television and cable services and turn to internet for your programming entertainment.

- If you live in an apartment, try downsizing or moving somewhere cheaper.

- Transfer high balances to new credit cards with lower APRs and lower your overall payback amount. However, careful not to gain a transfer fee higher than the % you could save.

- Educate yourself with blogs, documentaries, books. Research money managers and advice on getting out of debt. Some people have shows dedicated to helping people deal with debt.

- Put your mind to wealth, and think, "My actions are helping me think abundantly and contributing to my wealth." Instead of "I need to get out of debt" which is a lack mentality statement. You can't focus on debt and receive prosperity. You must focus on wealth while taking the actions towards it.

- Whenever you make some extra money, put it towards removing the debt. Don't spend it frivolously. The sacrifices now will pay off later.

- Keep a positive outlook and remember that being in any kind of debt is not optimal. You cannot freely live abundance when you are in the minus. You must take control of your financial situation right now and maintain your devotion to financial freedom. Imagine what it will feel like to finally be free of the invisible noose around your wallet?

- If you have extra time in your week, get a second side job and put all the money you make towards debts.

Which strategies of money management appeal to you?
___
___
___

Come up with your own fun and creative ways to save and invest:
___
___
___
___
___
___
___
___
___
___
___
___
___
___
___
___
___
___
___
___
___
___
___

DEBT Elimination - Work-Sheet

MONTHLY EXPENDITURES			
Office, work rent			
Renter's Insurance			
Home or Apt Repair			
Water/Sewer/Trash collection			
Household Toiletries/Groceries			
Landscaping			
Home mortgage or apartment rent			
Property taxes			
Home Repair and Association dues			
Haircuts/Self Care			
Car payment Car Insurance			
Other transportation costs			
Gas Auto			
Electric/Oil/Gas			
Heath/Life Insurance			
Laundry/Clothing/ Dry Cleaning			
Gifts and Donations			
Medicines/Doctor Expenses			

Entertainment including TV/Cable/Internet Fast food, eating out restaurant expenses Cellphone, pager Other expenses			
DEBTS OWED			
Home loans Student and education loans Car loans Child support and Alimony Credit Card debt			
INCOME			
Primary work or income: (career or job) Secondary income: Social Security, Retirement, Public assistance, Child support or Alimony Tertiary Income: (investment gains)			
EMERGENCY FUND			
In case of emergency only			
SAFETY - NEST EGG			
Income or investments you do not touch			

MY FINANCIAL STATUS

IN-VISION BOARD
CUT & PASTE PAGE

∽⑤∽⑤∽⑤

Look through magazines or get images from the internet that depict your financial status when you take control of your financial situation! What would you be able to buy? What would you be able to do? When all the money you earn is yours, how would that look and feel like?

∽⑤∽⑤∽⑤

> **Mental Manifestation Tip #10:**
>
> **Visualize getting a raise or a big boost in business.**

Whether you desire to make more money in your current position or desire to move up or get promoted, it's time to get clear on your professional goals. Once you know what you desire, add it to your In-Vision board at the end of this section.

Then, ask for that raise! Apply for that job! If you're afraid to ask, do your research to see what other people in a similar position are making or what sort of duties are expected in the new position. Know your worth and know what you desire. If you are unclear on your professional goals, spend some time journaling and developing your expectations. Then, manifest them!

Will do ☐ on date: _____ Completed ☐ on _____

Reflect on how this changed or improved your life:
_____

What fun and creative ways can you come up with for making money in your free time?
_____
_____
_____
_____
_____
_____
_____
_____
_____
_____
_____
_____
_____

MY PERFECT CAREER

IN-VISION BOARD
CUT & PASTE PAGE

ఆఆఆ

Look through magazines or get images from the internet that depict the perfect career for you. Do you have a boss or are you an entrepreneur? Are you the CEO of your own business? What does that flourishing business look like? What do your office desk and office look like? Where are you located? Where do you do business? Who are your customers? Do you work locally, nationally, or globally? What do you look like every day going to work? What are you wearing while there? Examine and create all the aspects of a successful, soon-to-be YOU!

ఆఆఆ

MY PERFECT TRANSPORTATION

IN-VISION BOARD
CUT & PASTE PAGE

◈◈◈◈

Look through magazines or get images from the internet that depict the perfect transportation in terms of your favorite automobile and other travel that your lifestyle will provide you. What type of car do you desire to drive? How do you fly to your vacation spots? Do you have a toy hobby ride, like a boat or helicopter, you enjoy outside of your usual work week's ride? It's your new life; start creating! Everything starts with a thought - it starts right here.

◈◈◈◈

> **Mental Manifestation Tip #11:**
> **Write a note to yourself in 5 years.**

While I say it's a note to yourself, the Universe will read it, too. Write a letter (written or typed, but I recommend written as there is the physical and visual dynamic that really drives it home) to your future self 5 years down the road.

Visualize the person you'll be then, what you'll have, and where you'll be when you're reading this letter. Tell yourself what your worries are now, as well as what you're grateful for. Tell yourself where you think you'll be in 5 years and what you visualize for the future. Be specific, be detailed, and don't worry – nobody else is going to read this but Future You!

Dishing out all of your concerns will give you clarity, especially when you think about yourself reading it 5 years from now. Will this bother you in 5 years? Probably not. Not only will it give you some perspective, it will also build those Mental Manifestation Muscles, too.

Will do ☐ on date: _____ Completed ☐ on _____

Reflect on how this changed or improved your life:
_____

> **Mental Manifestation Tip #12:**
> **Know when to say YES and when to say NO.**

Become a YES person to the right things. Become a NO person to the right things. While this is easier said than done, it generally involves finding what feels good and knowing what brings your vibration field down. Do you have friends that just make you feel great when you're around them? Say YES to hanging out with them more. Do you feel gross and sluggish when you go out late at night? Say NO to late nights!

Don't close off your opportunities by being negative or pessimistic. Just because you're saying NO to something doesn't mean it's innately bad or negative; it's just not ideal for you. This is part of being authentic with yourself – you have to be willing to let go of things that other people do so that you can conserve your energy for the things that most benefit you.

Will do ☐ on date: _____ Completed ☐ on _____

Reflect on how this changed or improved your life:

_____

> **Mental Manifestation Tip #13:**
> **Delete procrastination.**

Develop a DO IT NOW mentality. Mark Twain once said, *"Eat a live frog first thing in the morning and nothing worse will happen to you the rest of the day."* While I don't desire to eat a frog, the point is well made. It's a great way to break your procrastination habit. Do the hardest, most uncomfortable thing in the morning and the rest of your day will feel like a breeze.

The desire to procrastinate can also be a powerful tool in helping you understand your energy and what you truly desire to manifest. Are you procrastinating on writing that book? Maybe you don't desire to write a book; maybe you desire to make videos instead!

But by getting your work or tasks done when they should be done, you're showing the Universe that you are working towards your goals and not expecting everything to be handed to you on a silver platter.

Will do ☐ on date: _____ Completed ☐ on _____

Reflect on how this changed or improved your life:

_____

> **Mental Manifestation Tip #14:**
> **Permanently replace the words WANT, NEED and DECIDE in your vocabulary.**

If you desire to change your life in a big way quickly, reprogram these key words in your speaking. The words you speak have huge energy implications while presenting your underlying belief system's programming. We may unknowingly be hindering our authentic self by not meaning what we're saying. If you wish to get positive results, you must use positive words, feelings and actions - or you defeat yourself before even starting a task. I teach my clients to reprogram their self-talk by replacing the words want and need with the word DESIRE, and the word decide with the word CHOOSE. To want something hints to a mere superficial childish wish, rather than the strong deep feeling of desiring with the soul. Similarly, to need something notes lack and not feeling abundant. Therefore, desire is a much more powerful and positive word to use. The root cide stems from Latin meaning "killer or the act of killing," such as in the word suicide; to kill oneself. The root cide also means to have one side lose, giving victory to the other side. Example: The King had to decide which gladiator would die in the arena. No wonder those who have many abundant options but make decisions, feel they "lose out" to other activities in exchange for the one they pick. In contrast, "choose" means using your free will to pick one over the other not because of worth, but simply because of free personal preference. Example: Jane loves both strawberries and peaches, but today she chose to eat a peach; tomorrow she might eat a strawberry. Choosing leaves options open, while deciding kills off other options. Abundance never closes doors. If you are seeking better personal energy, proper use and feeling of your chosen words brings forth a much more pleasant reality.

Will do ☐ on date: _____ Completed ☐ on _____

Reflect on how this changed or improved your life:
_____

What negative slang (or cuss words of low vibration) can you remove and replace to empower your life?
_____
_____
_____
_____
_____
_____
_____
_____
_____
_____

A PRODUCTIVE DAY IN MY LIFE

IN-VISION BOARD
CUT & PASTE PAGE

Look through magazines or get images from the internet that highlight what your life would look like if you cut out all the useless parts of your day. What would a day in your life look like if you were more productive and more aligned with your authentic goals? Would you have more time for leisure? Would your office space be light and inviting? Would you have a better balance between home and work life? Choose only pictures that feel like your life once you've put aside procrastination and started working on your true purpose and direction!

CHAPTER FOUR:
CONNECTING WITH OUR AUTHENTIC SPIRIT

While many of us think the definition of spirit is simply "qualities that define us," this couldn't be further from the truth. Our spirit, and spirituality, is The Truth. It's Home. It's where each of us come from when we are born and will return to when we die. We are made in the image of our creator, and that is our true spirit.

So when I talk about having an authentic experience with "spirit," what do I mean? I mean knowing your home base, the truth of *you*. While we tell ourselves little lies our whole lives: "I'm too fat to be loved," "I'm too stupid to start my own business," "Nobody likes me" – spirit is where we all realize the truth. Spirit is what tells us "Keep going," "You ARE worthy," "You ARE going to do great things."

This is why I waited to introduce spirit until the end; once you have your body and mind on board, spirit is already waiting. Spirit is what is uncovered when you remove the junk from your body, the clutter from your mental space. Spirit is what you are left with when you get rid of all the STUFF the world tells you that you need.

Use the tasks and tips in this section to become really in tune with your spirit. There are a lot of exercises in this section to help you remove old traumas and bad energies so that your spirit can shine through.

4.1. Life Traumas for Neutralization

Taking your past issues that haunt your mind and subconscious and putting them onto a piece of paper will change the dynamics and how you deal with those issues. For many, it's the missing link to finding healing.

It is very important you take time out to complete this exercise FULLY. This means no distractions (turn off your cell phone, TV, radio, etc.). Value and love yourself enough to take time away. If you do this exercise halfway, while under stress, without focus or without care, it will reflect in your session's energy and in any expected results. Treat the time you devote to this exercise as sacred. **YES - it is that important.**

To do this worksheet, sit with your eyes closed in a restful, seated position with your pen in hand and on the paper. Do a meditation or prayer asking [your higher self/higher mind/God/guides/or angels] to bring forward any perceived blocks in your current life and any connection to past challenges into your conscious mind, so that you may put them on the paper and clear them in the session.

Clear your mind, let your higher spirit give you the answers as you ALLOW flow. Keep your eyes closed for a few minutes and feel anything that comes forward. See if you can view any scenarios or scenes play out in your mind's eye. You will gain pictures, images, ideas, and thoughts that will start to flood your mind. This is good, and it is how the higher mind answers your request. If you happen to blank out or feel like you cannot remember, this is because you are resisting or pushing too hard with your mental mind.

Open your eyes. Write anything that comes up according to each age. If you have difficulty with this exercise, let it go. Put it aside for another time when you are more relaxed and able to flow. Come back to it in a few hours or the next day. Try different parts of the day, as well. Some people find it easier at the end of the day while others feel it is easier once they wake up or are fresh out of meditation.

To fill out the worksheet, in each column, provide the necessary age and event/feeling correlations. Take the space you need per age to write what you need to get out. For this exercise, mention only the events, feelings, and ages where you had a negative traumatic charge or memory of something that bothered or still bothers you.

Sometimes, events happen over a span of years. In this circumstance, you may put in the age category ages grouped by bracket (Ex: [18-25]). Be as descriptive as possible with the feelings you felt. Events can be summarized by the most charged words and scenarios. However, DO NOT lessen or conceal anything you wish to deal with. The idea is to HEAL anything that is in the dark or shadows by exposing it to the light, thus freeing both you and your nervous system of it. Leave any ages without trauma unlisted. Start with Age 0 (birth) and end with your current age and events.

Connecting With Our Authentic Spirit

Life Story TimeLine - Kousouli Neural Emotive Reconditioning Work-Sheet KNER®

AGE	TRAUMATIC EVENT AS YOU REMEMBER IT	EMOTIONS YOU FELT WITH THE EVENT
0-5		
6		
7		
8		
etc.		

Copyright© Dr.Kousouli 2017 www.DrKousouli.Com All rights reserved. www.BEAMASTER.com

Life Story TimeLine - Kousouli Neural Emotive Reconditioning Work-Sheet KNER®

AGE	TRAUMATIC EVENT AS YOU REMEMBER IT	EMOTIONS YOU FELT WITH THE EVENT

Now look at what you wrote. This is your old story. This may be the story you continuously loop in your mind that you *think* defines you. In reality, though, it's just a bunch of events that occurred to reveal lessons and challenges to help you grow – no matter how hard the event was.

How does it feel now, looking back at the black and white pieces of paper and what you wrote? How can you look at these words and events in a new perspective? Can you forgive all involved in the making of these events? Can you - most importantly - forgive yourself?

You must if you desire to move forward with your life. When you write like this, you are clearing pathways for higher vibrations and making it possible for you to truly connect with your authenticity. It also makes it easier for you to get answers to those questions about who you truly are and what you're destined for, if only you know how to ask.

4.2 Divine Solutions Through the Hand

Sometimes in our lives, we bang our heads up against the wall for solutions and answers to our everyday dilemmas but still get no answers. We may have to look beyond the physical, into the higher mind, a place that science has now acknowledged its presence and its importance.

Even with all the intelligence and brain power available to us, we cannot deny that some of the most genius solutions, information, inventions, breakthroughs, or advice for our lives have come from the higher mind or some unseen spark of imagination or insight that created our masterpiece artwork, musical masterpieces, or gave us understanding of the human genome.

Psychography, also known as automatic writing, is a supernatural sixth sense which is believed to come from a spiritual or unseen force. The energy guides you to write words using your hand. Your hand transcribes information without you consciously writing or thinking about it. It is said that all higher mind or godly texts (such as the Gospels) have been written through psychography, by human minds inspired or influenced by Divine intervention.

I must admit, outside of actual book editing, much of my book series and methods were developed while I was deep in meditation, where I sat at my keyboard or at the library, just typing or writing away, oblivious to what was going on around me. I was laser targeted on downloading the bulk of information that was coming through me.

We all have abilities to connect to undeniable insight. With much practice, you can also receive enlightened information, even if it is a scribble or small word sent to you by your unseen higher vibratory guides or angels from the other side. Through meditation and prayer, you raise your vibration and your guides and angels lower their vibration to match our density here. We meet 'in the middle,' and that's how the process of communication is ultimately able to happen. Psychography sessions can be as long as a few seconds, minutes, or can go on for hours depending on your focused intention, how open to the connection you are, and the information coming through.

I must stress that success has 100% to do with feeling deserving of the process and holding the loving intention to receive information clear of doubt, fear, or worry. The arms are spiritually connected to the heart chakra. Your heart chakra holds the truth that powers the energy coming through, so of course you should get yourself into a state of love when practicing auto-writing.

Tapping Into the Higher Self Through Automatic Writing

The process is safe, simple, and straightforward so don't over complicate it. You will need a pen, pencil, and blank sheet of paper on a hard surface. Some pages are left blank after this section for you to start practicing on. Sit in a comfortable chair with back support and hold the pen or pencil in your dominant hand and put it to the paper in anticipation of writing. Hold the point to the paper, then meditate and pray as you would normally do; I recommend doing the meditation and prayer process as I teach it in **BE A MASTER® OF PSYCHIC ENERGY**, as I have found that works well for my students. I should remind you, meditation and prayer are distinctly different. Meditation helps clear the mind. Prayer helps create the abundance or result of your asking by connecting to that which you seek through loving gratitude.

Do not skip the protection prayer prior to starting your meditation. Requesting with strong intent that your archangels clear your space from any negative influences, thoughts, vibrations, etc. is paramount to receiving high level information. Otherwise your session could be interfered with by less-than-suitable vibrations, which I also explain in depth in **BE A MASTER® OF PSYCHIC ENERGY**.

As you are in a state of meditative bliss, ask your question(s). It may take you a while to receive anything and it can be very frustrating when you first start. For some, answers come very easily, while others struggle. I find this to be true of those who have a hard time with life direction and feel little joy, or those who are blocking themselves by feeling undeserving, unloved, and critical of themselves. The more un-authentic, fake, and removed from their child-like joy they are, the harder anything concerning psychic phenomenon and esoteric ability seems to be. So, approach this with a child-like imaginative, adventurous essence – allow yourself to be free. Any bit of negativity, doubt or cynicism in your mind or heart, and you'll be guaranteed of no results. You can't trick yourself into believing and you can't lie to your soul. You must be authentic.

A good time length for a session of automatic writing can be as little as 5 minutes to a half hour. However, it will depend on how much your higher self or guide desires to connect to give you your message. The pen or pencil will seem to move on its own with no effort; the things being written you will know are not from your conscious mind. It feels as if someone lovingly takes your hand and writes for you. It's not heavy, it's light and swift, gentle and very airy. You really feel as if the question you had in your heart not only has been answered, but you will also feel a deep gratitude for the way that message came to you.

You must be sensitive to all communication, such as random music playing in the background that gives you an important message, or number and letter sequences that are meaningful to you, such as a birthday or spelling of a name. You must pay close attention when you start reaching out to the other side. This is especially important when chance synchronicities start to occur in your life. Guides and angels are very subtle with you; they don't desire to scare you by showing up abruptly. Synchronicities are key signals that you are starting to make a connection. Automatic writing can be a skill you develop later, after you have paid attention to the subtle cues in your life that your guides and angels are using to get your attention. Don't give up.

If you're new to spiritual communication, automatic writing may be challenging without understanding the basis described in **BE A MASTER® OF PSYCHIC ENERGY**. You may wish to have that solid base knowledge prior to attempting this and any other intuitive process mentioned. It would be very helpful in understanding how everything works and why this process is viable for your life's unfolding journey for tapping into valuable soul exploration.

_____

_____

_____

_____

_____

_____

_____

_____

4.3 Locate Negative Vibes

One thing you should never underestimate on your journey to an amazing life is the power bad energy can have on your body, spirit, mind, and emotions. It takes spiritual intuition and evaluation to really look at your energy levels and see where there are negative influences worming their way into your being.

In this fun but important exercise, using aspects of the Kousouli® Method we help pinpoint areas of energy congestion, which may show up as spiritual, mental, emotional, and physical intrusions. These are the unseen forces that cause very tangible real issues with our day-to-day lives.

In each body figure, you will shade in areas where you get a 'nudge' or sense of an area that may need attention. Meditate and focus your mind in the various categories. Start with Spiritual, then go in order of Mental, Emotional, and Physical. You can use colored pencils or pens to shade in any areas that you may feel hold negative energy. If you don't know, sit still and meditate, simply asking your higher self: "Spiritually, where am I holding onto foreign energies that are not my original self?" You will get a nudge that indicates your neck or lower abdominal area.

Then ask your higher self, "What color is this energy vibration?" And you may get an impression of black or dark blue. Shade in that area with the color you feel it is. Repeat with the other layers - Mental, Emotional and Physical. "Mentally, where in my body am I holding onto foreign energies that are not my original self?" And then Emotionally: "Emotionally, where in my body am I holding onto foreign energies that are not my original self and causing me strife?" Physical is the easiest, as any tension, pain, or aching will easily show up for you.

Color each area what your intuition tells you. You cannot get it wrong, and your aura is a dynamic environment. The way it feels in one moment will change in a different time and moment. It is wise to do this exercise several times throughout this month and over the course of a year to see what is still there and what has lifted or been made lighter with self-work over time.

Meditate on removing the energy and erasing it, as if you have a magic sponge.

How do I remove this negative energy?

When removing negative energy from your auric field, envision it as a small chunk of eggshell that fell into your pan. Of course, you don't want that little piece of shell floating around! So you take it out of the pan. This is just like what you'd do with the negative energy – you carefully, with focus, remove it from your auric field.

What kind of energy should I remove?

There are four main categories of **TOXIC resistance** that can keep people from being more authentic. While you may not see them as negative in the moment, you will once you look at these emotions more objectively. The worst part about negativity is that it lies to us and tells us that it feels *good* to feel negative.

This couldn't be further from the truth. Let's work on removing:

1. Blame. Blaming yourself, others or something else; You play the part of a martyr or embody the victim mentality. This blocks you from receiving positive energy.

2. Self-pity. A false sense of self-nurturing, usually from childhood, usually involving blame again. This goes deeper though, and affects your ability to positively engage with positive energy.

3. Lack of self-responsibility or willingness. Avoidance of self-empowerment and responsibility; inability to just "own it." You often don't hold yourself accountable to anyone or anything if it doesn't benefit you.

4. Clinging to the past. A traumatic past life, old beliefs, subconscious issues from your youth or current life, can all cloud your energy NOW.

Once you've done your auric scan and assessed the color of your energy on a physical, spiritual, mental, and emotional level, you'll be ready to address the REAL you underneath all that grime. You are the window; you see your world through your interactions with energy. If you look through a dirty window, you can't see! Get some spiritual Windex on there and get really clear on who you are and what you desire. Only now can you be truly authentic. After spending some time meditating and asking honestly your higher mind to show you the current representation of what your energies look like.

In the following pages, use color pencils and draw in where in your energy field or body you see any of the specific energies just discussed above. Are they colorful, vibrant? Or are there any murky, darker areas lingering? Is your chest feeling/looking heavy? Be honest with yourself and where these lesser flowing energies may be bothering your field. On every page, Spiritual, Mental, Emotional, and Physical – depict it just as you envision it in your mind.

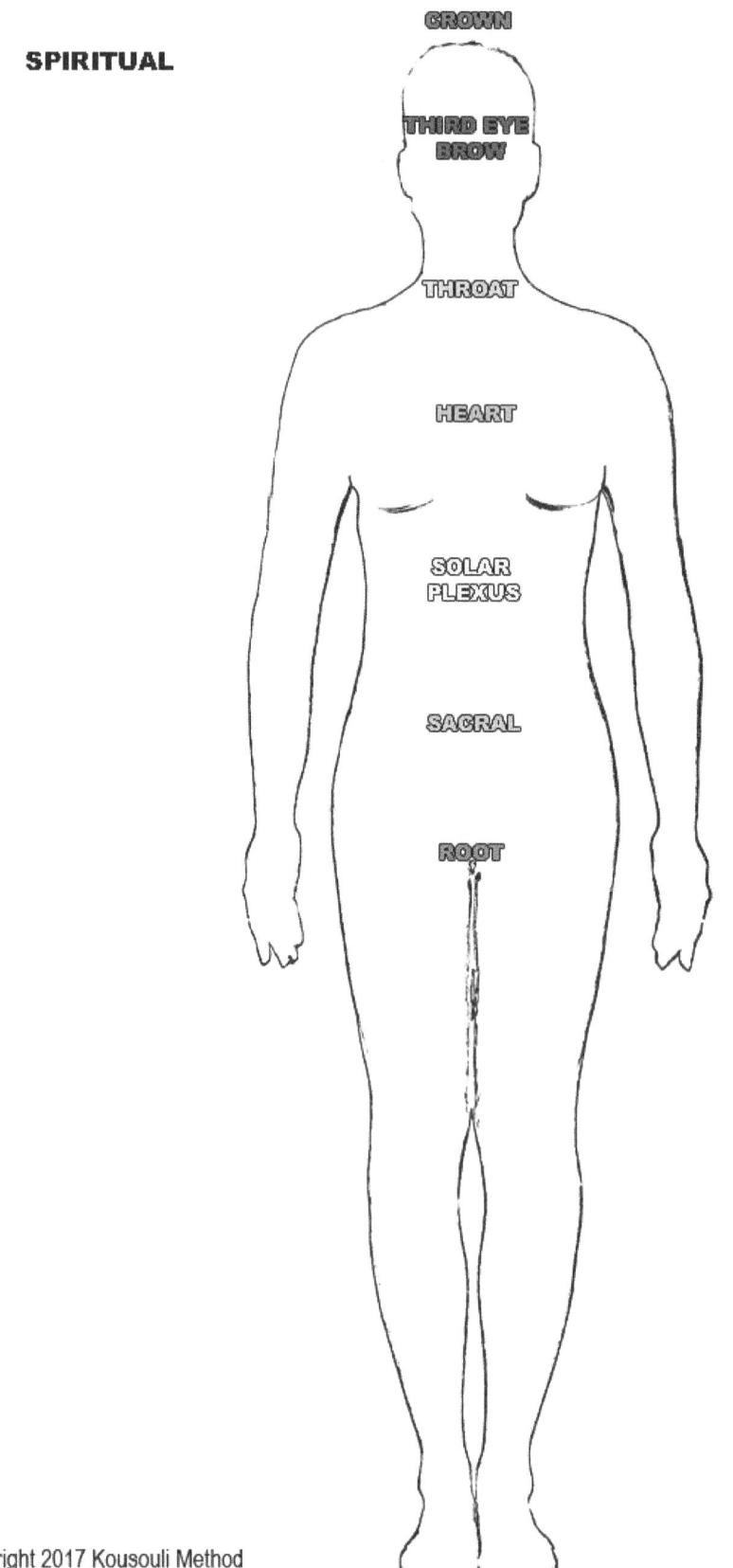

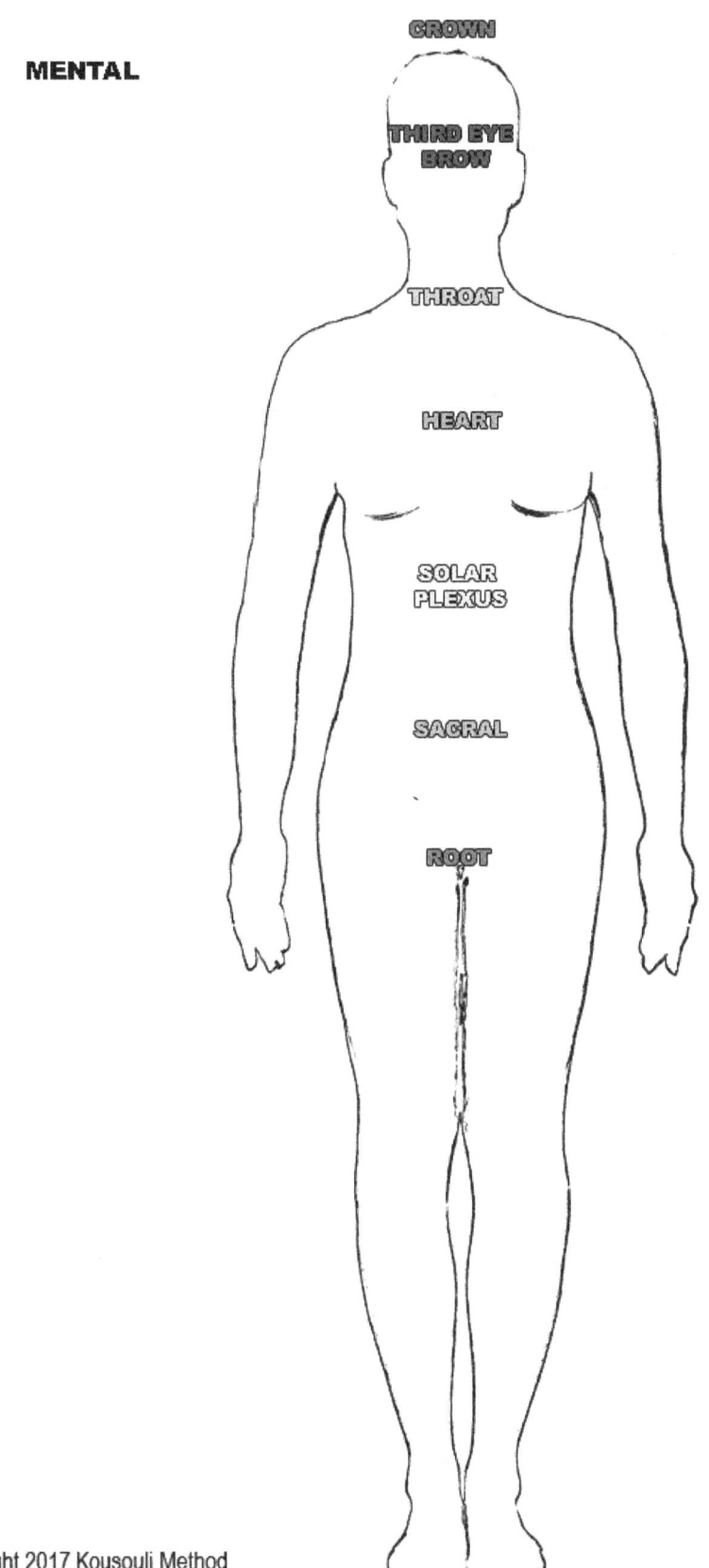

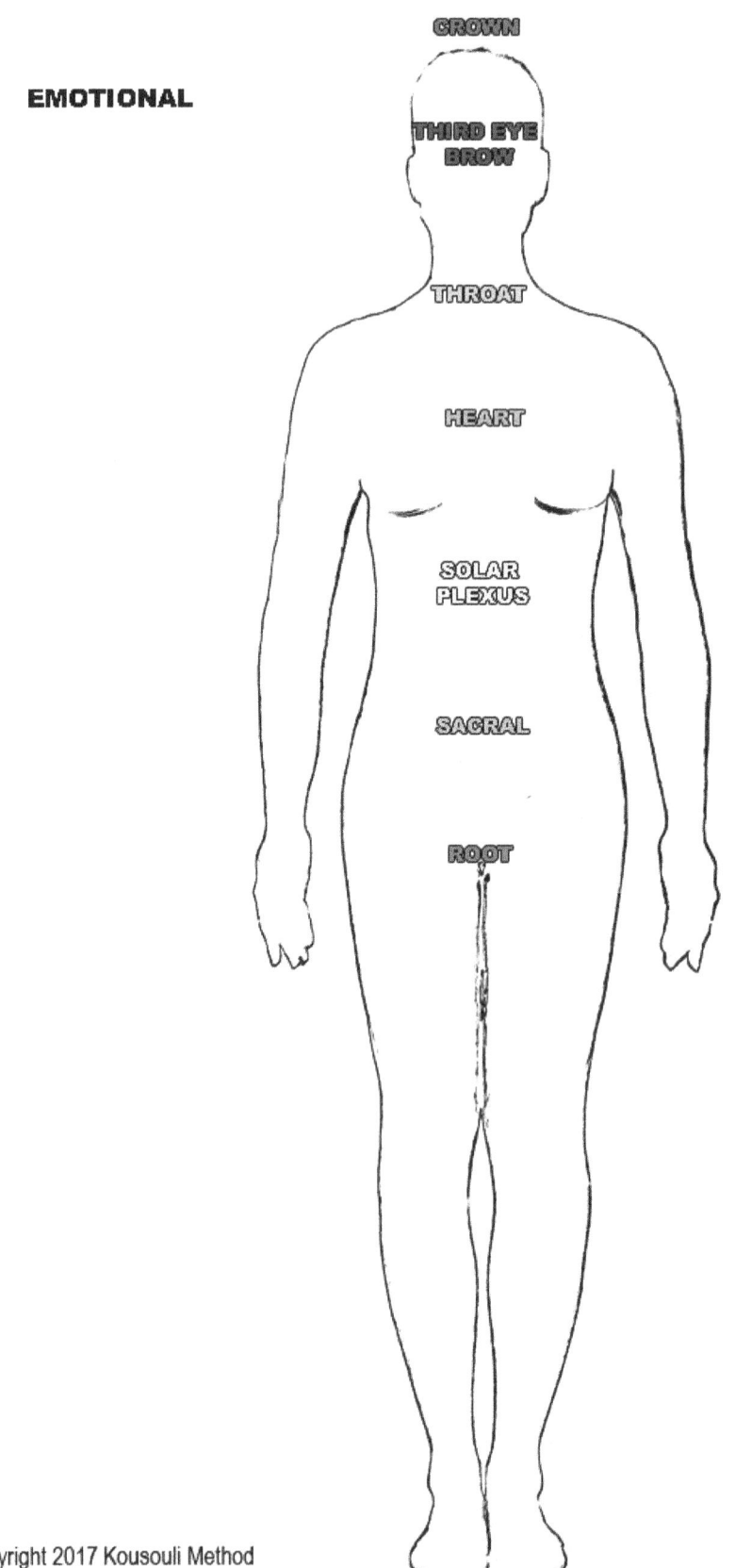

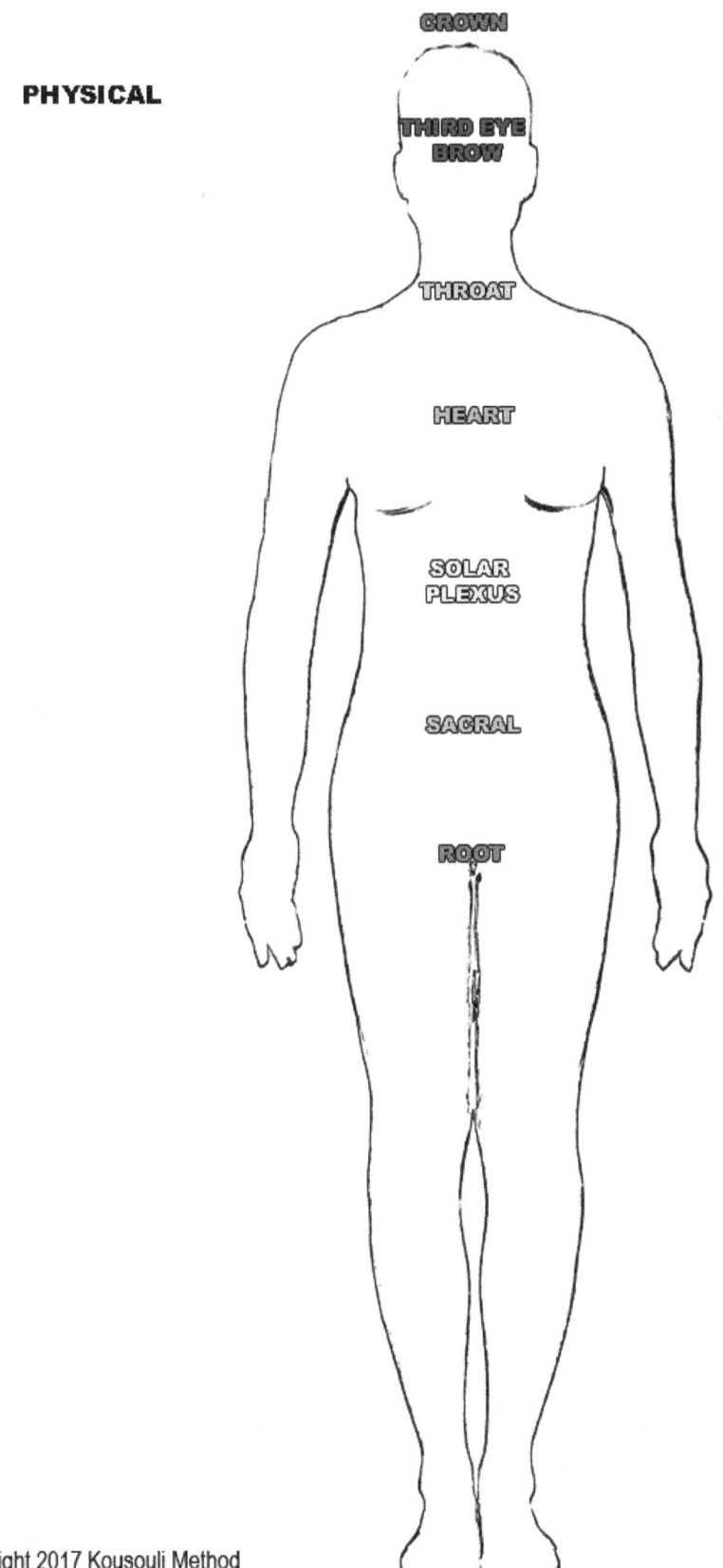

In the next two images, draw what your combined energies (combined spiritual, mental, emotional and physical) look like in your aura.

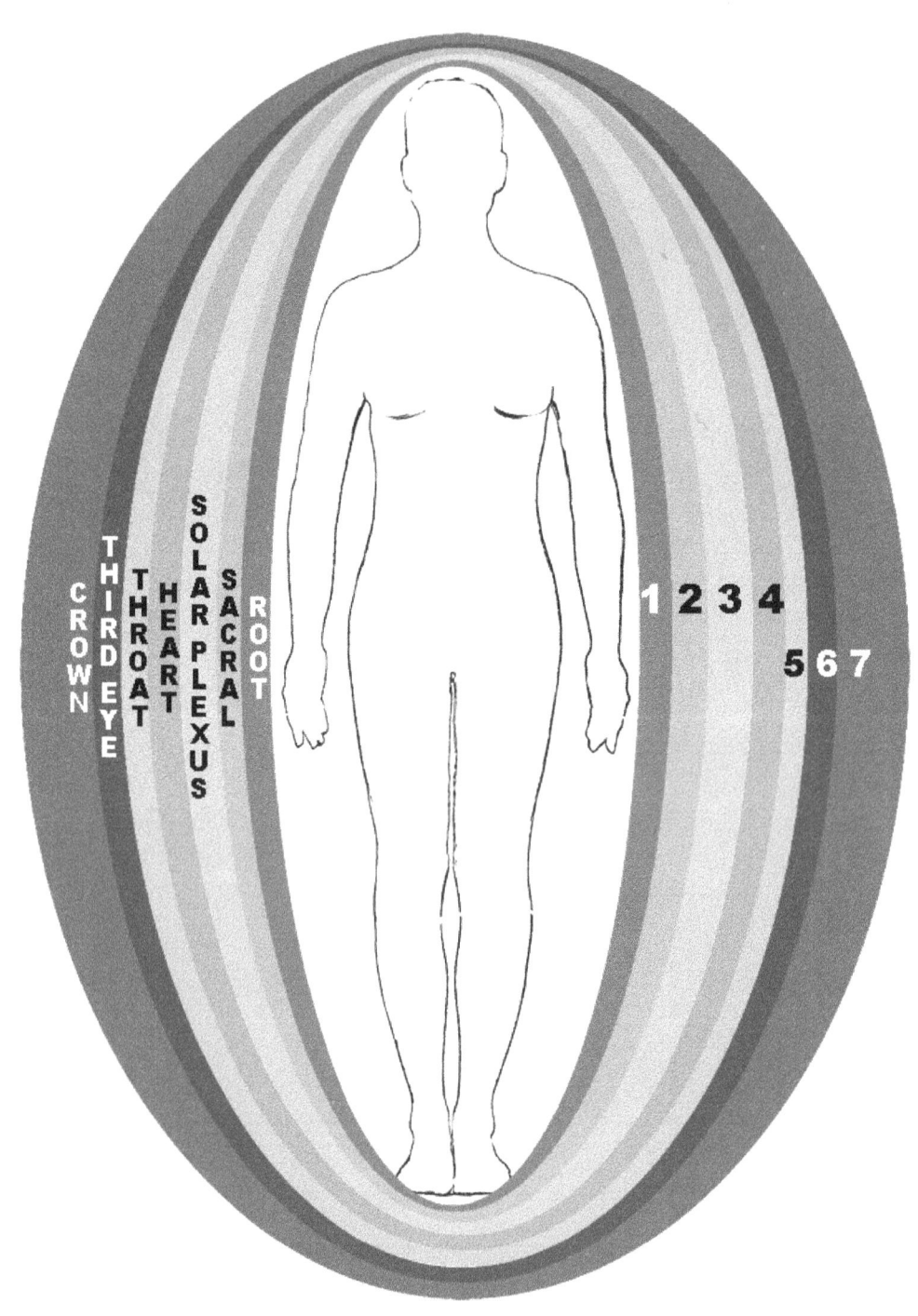

Copyright 2017 Kousouli Method

Connecting With Our Authentic Spirit

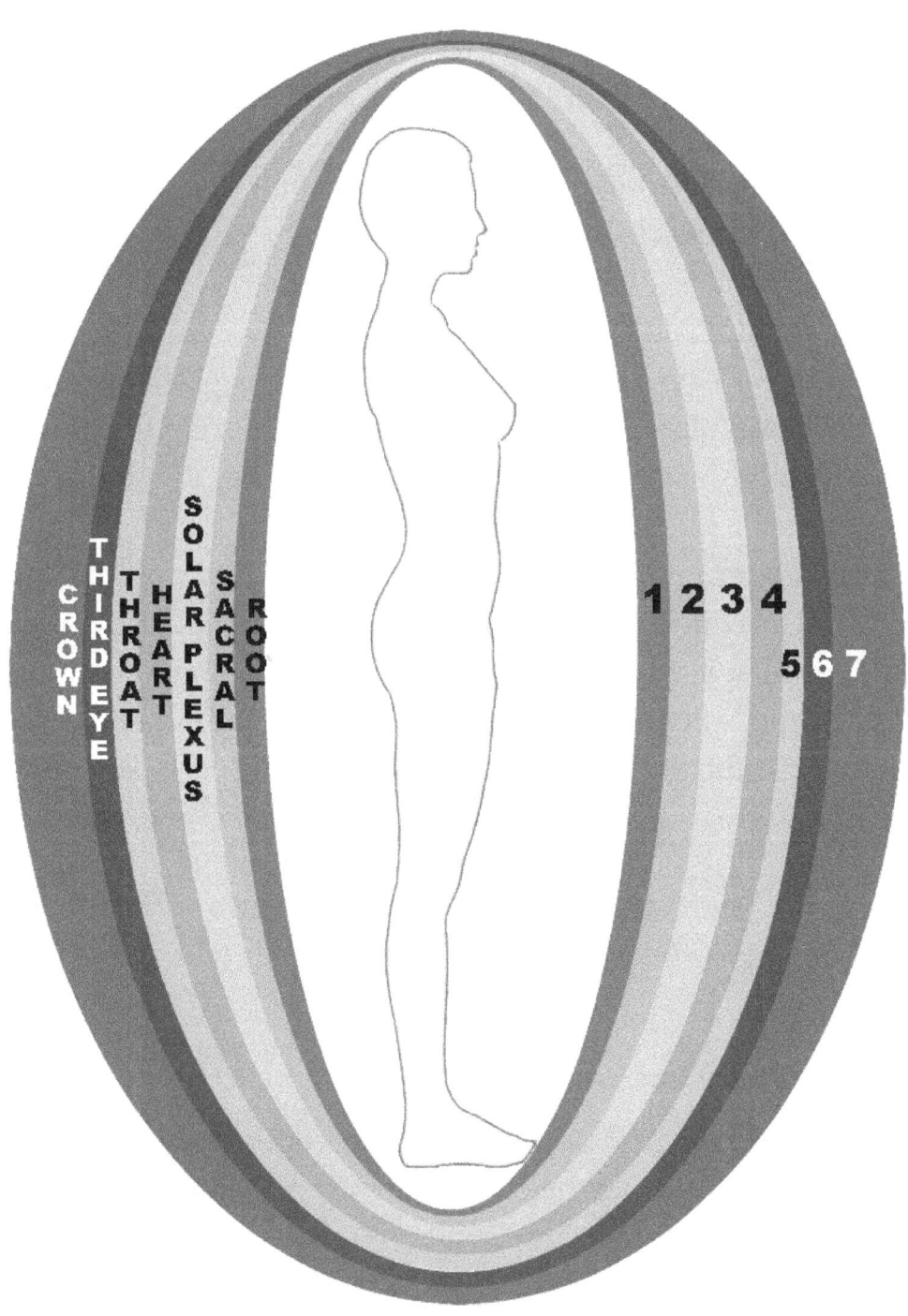

Copyright 2017 Kousouli Method

4.4 Recognize and Remove Negative Vibes and Negative People

The last component of your authenticity journey is going to be recognizing the energy of the world and people around you. What if you've become "enlightened" about who you are, but are still surrounded by people who seek to bring you back to their way of doing things? How are you going to ever grow if you're constantly being held back?

People, in general, are good natured, given that their basic needs of food, clothing, and shelter are met. People don't seek to harm others, at least not intentionally. Negative thoughts, however, do, and they creep into the minds of good people through generational traditions, customs, and repetition. Babies, for instance, are not born racists, but given a few years living in a racist family, those thoughts creep into their little heads every time.

Because you cannot directly *see* thoughts, it's important to recognize them in actions. Studying human nature and how people behave is probably one of the most "a-ha!" skills you can acquire in your roadmap to an amazing life. Since everything centers around relationships, there are few key types of negativity that you can learn to recognize and avoid.

Many people harbor negative energy from long standing chronic thought patterns, and these will often manifest into tangible physical characteristics and behaviors. These can tip you off at parties, as an employer, or if gauging a new potential mate. Avoiding these people will save you headaches, energy drains and keep you moving on your path to authenticity.

The 'Got an Excuse for Everything' Type

"Sorry I'm late traffic was crazy!," "My dog ate my homework," "She started it!" This person is always weaseling out of everything because they take zero responsibility for their actions.

The 'Lack is Everywhere But in Me' Type

It's never their fault. It's never their bad idea. They continuously see others as the issue, not understanding that what they think and how they act is their world and their world is reflecting right back at themselves.

The 'Bully' Type

These kinds use physical and emotional intimidation to get their way. Truth is, inside they are victims of the same pain they inflict. You have probably been avoiding this person for a long time, anyways, so just make the avoidance permanent.

The 'Gossip Girl' Type

The Gossip Girl is one of the most cunning in the negativity game. They use gossip as a weapon to distort truths, make and break alliances, or trap others into their game. While you will undoubtedly be a source of gossip for them as you remove yourself from their web, you'll feel an immediate relief of negativity when you do.

The 'Debbie- Downer' Type

No matter the party or celebration, the Debbie Downer always brings up the smallest issue and makes it a big deal. Always seeing the glass as half empty, these people just suck the joy out of life. It's not your job to help this person, especially not at the risk of your new spiritual progress.

The 'Know It all' Type

These people remind you that they are the smartest in the bunch. In reality, though, they are just the smart–*asses* of the bunch and the way they treat people stinks. They are ego-centered and seek to show superiority in the group by putting others down.

The 'Do Just Enough to Get By' Type

These people have laziness down to a science. They do just enough not to get fired, just enough not to flunk the class, just enough to make the room clean enough that their parent or spouse doesn't yell at them…These people hardly escalate past average. Avoid them.

The 'Tit for Tat' Type

These people will use their looks, influence, connections, and 'favors' to bring you into their debt. "I did this for you, what will you do for me?" is a common refrain. They are toxic, especially when they get into a relationship, as they keep scores and live in a world of conditional, insincere love. This is the exact opposite of authenticity.

The 'Control Freak' Type

This person must always interrupt conversations by not letting someone finish their sentences, and uses "I" a lot. You'll notice they make the plans, want to be involved in everything, and always have an opinion on what you're doing. Your authentic self doesn't have time to let someone else take control; disengage ASAP.

The 'Energy Vampire' Type

Usually those being bitten by the energy vampire will never know until it's too late. You can gauge this one by the lack of productivity and a feeling of sudden sleepiness, brain fogginess, headache, irritability, or a need to rehydrate after spending time with someone. This won't get better; avoid interacting with this person!

4.5 Avoid, Disengage, and Grow Your Positive Posse

Do you know of any of these negative people? Are you reading any of these and thinking "Oh my God, I think I might be one of these negative people!" Don't worry – it's not too late. Look at going to the source of the problem – "your old programming". With an in-depth look at who you are and why you may be acting that way, you can quickly reroute that behavior and begin to work on the problem at hand.

If it's a friend or someone in your group of friends that embodies one of the negative personality types, this next exercise may give you some insight into healing by putting the thoughts into words for the examination of the self. It's so important to let go of any judgement on yourself and others, and also learn to forgive yourself. It's time to start attracting people with higher vibrational patterns so that you can remain true to your authentic self and so you can make the world a better place – person by person!

Seek Those Good, Good Vibrations

People with good vibrations are just the opposite of all the previous descriptions. They give positive feedback, don't criticize, connect to other's needs compassionately, are helpful, love others, and are a joy to be around. They literally light up the room when they walk in.

These people are GOLD to your spiritual development, and when you are sensitive enough to see these people, being around them will energize and stimulate your life. I try to always surround myself with these types of people as they make life so much more enjoyable. They say that the five people you spend the most time with is the sum of what and who you will become. This is so true.

Your growth and life can literally change overnight when you add the energy of a few good people into your field. Most of the time, you can't find out who you are if you are still balancing out negative friends and relatives. Your authentic self may have some serious negative vibes thrown at it. And, like wet dirt, it will crust over and hide the hidden gem's (your authentic self's) luster inside.

Over time, the layers of negativity and vibratory sludge get so thick that you have no idea why you are feeling so down, anxious, sad, or worried when you know you're a happy and good person. And this is all because you didn't avoid the negativity of those around you.

Choose your peers wisely, as they define who you become! This is the biggest component to spiritual authenticity; knowing yourself well enough to know who is worthy of your presence and love.

4.6 Meet like-minded positive people at workshops and seminars

Speaking of good vibrations; when like-minded individuals find each other at my seminars the energy is amazing! Great friendships are made and long term relationships are forever forged. Countless times I have heard feedback from attendees who claim they have finally found their "tribe" after decades of feeling like no one understood them. Of course I love this! It fuels my purpose of bringing people together for personal empowerment even more. Positive energy is like that - it drives people to do more and become a better version of themselves every day.

Self help seminars and workshops inspire people, like yourself, who are powerfully transforming their lives. These events bring together a supportive community and loving sense of understanding that you are not alone in the world; many others are sharing in your challenges and story of self discovery. For more information on upcoming seminars sign up for our FREE newsletter lists at *www.KousouliMethod.com* and *www.BeAMaster.com*

CHAPTER FIVE

DAILY ACTS OF SELF CARE

How often do you take time out to just take care of yourself? You run around, gather the kids from school, take care of aging parents, or work your tail off, but you don't ever take time for yourself. If this sounds about right, you'll take the most away from this next section. I recommend *really* sticking to the recommendations here, checking them off and building them into your schedule. Only when you take care of yourself can you take care of those around you.

Self Care Tip #1:

Electronic detox.

Challenge yourself to turn off the Television, Internet, Cell Phones, all electronics for 1 weekend. Spend some time with nature camping or strolling the beach.

Will do ☐ on date: _____ Completed ☐ on _____

Reflect on how this changed or improved your life:

_____

Self Care Tip #2:

Touch base.

Talk to someone you have not talked to in a while. This could be someone you don't like or it could just be someone who has been out of touch for a while. Mend fences and rebuild bridges.

Will do ☐ on date: _____ Completed ☐ on _____

Reflect on how this changed or improved your life:

_____

Friends you can invite to do this activity with:

_____

Self Care Tip #3:
Call in sick.

Take a sick day when you're not sick and do absolutely nothing. While this may seem lazy, it's actually the highest form of self-care there is. Taking time to be with yourself and to do absolutely nothing. Best activity: clear your mind and meditate.

Will do ☐ on date: _____ Completed ☐ on _____

Reflect on how this changed or improved your life:

_____

Self Care Tip #4:
Fall in love with podcasts.

Find a great podcast to download to your computer or phone. There are millions out there, from politics to self-improvement to short stories to comedy.

Will do ☐ on date: _____ Completed ☐ on _____

Reflect on how this changed or improved your life:

_____

Self Care Tip #5:
The Internet is for cat videos.

Find a funny cat video on YouTube and share in social media. Everyone loves funny animal videos.

Will do ☐ on date: _____ Completed ☐ on _____

Reflect on how this changed or improved your life:

_____

Self Care Tip #6:
Admit your ignorance.

Say "I don't know, but will find out" more. This is hard for so many of us because admitting that we don't know can make us feel inferior to people around us. But by saying "I don't know, but will find out" more, we're giving ourselves a list of things we have so much to learn about!

Will do ☐ on date: _____ Completed ☐ on _____

Reflect on how this changed or improved your life:

_____

Self Care Tip #7:
Say you're sorry.

Apologize to someone you have wronged. This takes an act of absolute humbleness, but you will feel renewed once it is over.

Will do ☐ on date: _____ Completed ☐ on _____

Reflect on how this changed or improved your life:

_____

Friends you can invite to do this activity with:

_____

Self Care Tip #8:
Schedule a game night.

Plan a game night with friends or family. Have each person bring a game or go buy a couple if you can. Leave your phones at the door and just enjoy each other's company.

Will do ☐ on date: _____ Completed ☐ on _____

Reflect on how this changed or improved your life:
_____

Friends you can invite to do this activity with:
_____

> ### Self Care Tip #9:
> ### Cut the cord.

Cut the cable on your TV. For some, this may seem a bold move. For others, it may not be so hard. Turn the cable off on your TV if you can't cancel it entirely and spend more time outside, reading, exercising, cooking, or being with your family.

Will do ☐ on date: _____ Completed ☐ on _____

Reflect on how this changed or improved your life:
_____

> ### Self Care Tip #10:
> ### Time for a dance party.

Listen to an old mix tape or CD you've had for years. Don't be afraid to dance around the house.

Will do ☐ on date: _____ Completed ☐ on _____

Reflect on how this changed or improved your life:
_____

> ### Self Care Tip #11:
> ### Apps are the enemy.

Delete unproductive social media apps from your phone and see how much more productive you are. If you need the apps for work (or just don't want to give them up), move them to a new area of your phone and put a podcast or e-book app in their place. This way, when you open your phone, you are automatically giving yourself a way to learn something new instead of get sucked into social media.

Will do ☐ on date: _____ Completed ☐ on _____

Reflect on how this changed or improved your life:

_____

Self Care Tip #12:
Wear colors.

Stop wearing dark clothes (especially all black). Wear colorful clothes that reflect the energy you truly desire to embody.

- Deep red for vitality, energy
- Red for competitive spirit, winning
- Orange for adventure
- Deep yellow for academic, logical
- Yellow for energetic and creative
- Green for social, harmonious

Will do ☐ on date: _____ Completed ☐ on _____

Reflect on how this changed or improved your life:

_____

Self Care Tip #13:
Meditate with music to focus or attend a local 'sound bath' event.

Listen to calm classical music or white noise to help you focus. Also try to listen to upbeat, positive music as what you listen to can affect your mood and thoughts.

Will do ☐ on date: _____ Completed ☐ on _____

Reflect on how this changed or improved your life:

_____

Self Care Tip #14:
Achieve Inbox Zero.

Declutter your email inbox. Delete old email threads you don't need, organize your saved emails in folders, and unsubscribe from sites you don't like anymore.

Will do ☐ on date: _____ Completed ☐ on _____

Reflect on how this changed or improved your life:
_____

Self Care Tip #15:
Rent a funny movie.

Watch a comedy movie, new or old. Laughter is, after all, the best medicine.

Will do ☐ on date: _____ Completed ☐ on _____

Reflect on how this changed or improved your life:
_____

Friends you can invite to do this activity with:
_____

Self Care Tip #16:
Make your bed.

Always make your bed when you get out of it. That will set the tone for your day, you'll already feel accomplished and you'll come home to an inviting bed.

Will do ☐ on date: _____ Completed ☐ on _____

Reflect on how this changed or improved your life:
_____

Self Care Tip #17:
Go see a comedy show.

Buy tickets to see a comedian perform with your closest friends. Not only will you be happy to have a night out, but you'll be with people you love, laughing your heads off.

Will do ☐ on date: _____ Completed ☐ on _____

Reflect on how this changed or improved your life:
_____

Friends you can invite to do this activity with:
_____

Self Care Tip #18:
Buy the art.

Invest in your home and positive energy by purchasing artwork or decorations created by artists you love.

Will do ☐ on date: _____ Completed ☐ on _____

Reflect on how this changed or improved your life:
_____

Self Care Tip #19:
Make your house a haven.

Paint one accent room in your house, apartment, or office (if you can) a color that motivates and invigorates you.

- Blue = calming
- Orange = expands creativity
- Green = money, success

- Purple = spirituality
- Yellow = focus, cheer
- Deep red = passion

Will do ☐ on date: _____ Completed ☐ on _____

Reflect on how this changed or improved your life:
_____

Friends you can invite to do this activity with:
_____

Self Care Tip #20:
Take a trip down Memory Lane.

Go through old photos of yourself and your family. Save your favorites, make copies for others, and create gifts like scrapbooks or frames that you can give for birthdays or holidays.

Will do ☐ on date: _____ Completed ☐ on _____

Reflect on how this changed or improved your life:
_____

Self Care Tip #21:
Check out a TED Talk.

Watch TED Talks about a variety of subjects; the brain, psychology, the environment. You can learn so much from a 15-minute TED Talk!

Will do ☐ on date: _____ Completed ☐ on _____

Reflect on how this changed or improved your life:
_____

Friends you can invite to do this activity with:
_____

Self Care Tip #22:
Exercise your brain.

Whenever you have downtime, instead of picking up your phone or turning on the TV, try to do a Sudoku puzzle or a crossword. This is a great way to develop more connections in your brain, which has actually been proven to fight off dementia and brain dysfunction as we age.

Will do ☐ on date: _____ Completed ☐ on _____

Reflect on how this changed or improved your life:

_____

Self Care Tip #23:
Get a new haircut and put on some new shoes.

Buy a pair of new comfortable shoes. It doesn't matter whether they're tennis shoes, heels, or neon green flip-flops. There's just something about new shoes and a new haircut that make a person feel good. Maybe they will take you to new places.

Will do ☐ on date: _____ Completed ☐ on _____

Reflect on how this changed or improved your life:

_____

Self Care Tip #24:
Have a loud music party.

Wait until you're having a bad day (unfortunately such a day seems to always come) and find the loudest rock or punk station you can find on the radio, online, or from an old playlist. **Crank it up, dance** and **let the bad vibes go!**

Will do ☐ on date: _____ Completed ☐ on _____

Reflect on how this changed or improved your life:

_____

CHAPTER SIX:
RANDOM ACTS OF KINDNESS

This chapter really speaks for itself. When you raise your own authenticity, you desire to see the authenticity and the joy in the world around you. Here are a few of my favorite ways to show the world your truest, most joyful self.

> **Random Act of Kindness #1:**
> **Talk to a homeless person.**

As a society, we tend to shy away from these individuals because we assume they are degenerates, drunks, or mentally ill. But the #1 thing that homeless people need according to humanitarian studies is not money or a home – it's to be *seen*. Make eye contact and start a conversation. You'll both be changed.

Will do ☐ on date: _____ Completed ☐ on _____

Reflect on how this changed or improved your life:
_____

Friends you can invite to do this activity with:
_____

> **Random Act of Kindness #2:**
> **Plant a tree or help build a community garden.**

Get dirty and help grow something that will save the environment – maybe even feed people!

Will do ☐ on date: _____ Completed ☐ on _____

Reflect on how this changed or improved your life:
_____

Friends you can invite to do this activity with:
_____

> ### Random Act of Kindness #3:
> ### Hug it out.

Hug someone who needs it, and hug them a few seconds longer than you normally would. Human contact is some of the most healing power in this universe. Always hug heart to heart. It's a much more powerful hug. Try it!

Will do ☐ on date: _____ Completed ☐ on _____

Reflect on how this changed or improved your life:
_____

Friends you can invite to do this activity with:
_____

> ### Random Act of Kindness #4:
> ### Be polite.

Remember the rules of politeness that you learned in Kindergarten. You're never too old to say "Please," "Thank you," "Bless you," or "Excuse me." Also hold open the door for people behind you, let people merge in front of you on the highway, and help people carry something heavy. Kindness is healing.

Will do ☐ on date: _____ Completed ☐ on _____

Reflect on how this changed or improved your life:
_____

> ### Random Act of Kindness #5:
> ### Respect your elders.

Volunteer in a retirement community or nursing home. Not only will you have more respect for your elders, but they love the company.

Will do ☐ on date: _____ Completed ☐ on _____

Reflect on how this changed or improved your life:
_____

Friends you can invite to do this activity with:
_____

> **Random Act of Kindness #6:**
>
> **Help out man's best friend.**

Go to an animal shelter (if you're not allergic to animals) and volunteer to walk the puppies or even pet the cats. Nothing can boost your mood like loving an animal for a little while, and shelters need all the help they can get.

Will do ☐ on date: _____ Completed ☐ on _____

Reflect on how this changed or improved your life:
_____

Friends you can invite to do this activity with:
_____

> **Random Act of Kindness #7:**
>
> **Spend the day with a child.**

Hang out with a child for a day, whether a friend's toddler or a niece or nephew if you don't have children of your own. Sign up to be a Big Brother or a Big Sister with the Big Brothers and Sisters of America. Play with kids, talk to them, and think like them. A child's world is the most innocent place to be and will remind you of what's really important.

Will do ☐ on date: _____ Completed ☐ on _____

Reflect on how this changed or improved your life:
_____

> **Random Act of Kindness #8:**
>
> **Pay it forward.**

Pay for the person behind you at the drive thru, coffee shop, or café next time. Hopefully they will pay it forward, but either way you have invoked the Law of Abundance (and probably made their day).

Will do ☐ on date: _____ Completed ☐ on _____

Reflect on how this changed or improved your life:
_____

Come up with new fun ways to express random acts of kindness:
_____
_____
_____
_____
_____
_____
_____
_____
_____
_____
_____
_____
_____
_____
_____
_____

CHAPTER SEVEN:
NOVELTY KEEPS US YOUNG

In this final section of the book, I'd like to introduce you to the authentic, joyful self you've crafted over the last hundred plus pages. Congratulations on making it this far. Now, I think it's time to have a little bit more fun. Did you know that novel things, even like taking a different route to work in the morning and playing a new game of trivia can connect new pathways in your brain? Studies show that this neural activity cuts off dis-ease, like Alzheimer's and dementia, as we age and actually helps us live longer!

Novelty is the spice of life, so go do something new and exciting!

Novelty Tip #1:

Drastically change your daily routine.

Get up earlier, eat different food, try new shops, a new favorite tea, and move your desk around at work. Shake things up a bit; variety is the spice of life.

Will do ☐ on date: _____ Completed ☐ on _____

Reflect on how this changed or improved your life:

_____

Novelty Tip #2:

Learn a new language.

Use apps, computer programs, or videos. Studies find that brains actually act differently when we speak in different languages; they literally rewire our cognitive function! This helps your brain develop in whole new ways, keeps your brain healthy as you age, and also makes you a really fun guest at parties (all over the world)!

Will do ☐ on date: _____ Completed ☐ on _____

Reflect on how this changed or improved your life:

_____

Friends you can invite to do this activity with:

_____

> ### Novelty Tip #3:
> ### Save up to travel to a new country.

Travel has been proven to keep us healthy because we walk, hike, swim when we go on vacation, but also because we reduce our stress levels. Cortisol can kill, given enough time. Travel also opens your mind up to new ideas and lifestyles – the world is not limited to your experiences.

Do your research to see where you desire to go, how much it'll cost to get there, and where'll you stay once you do. This will help you plan for your trip and save accordingly. Make it happen in the next 365 days – you can do it!

Will do ☐ on date: _____ Completed ☐ on _____

Reflect on how this changed or improved your life:

_____

Friends you can invite to do this activity with:

_____

> ### Novelty Tip #4:
> ### Read self-help books.

I recommend the BE A MASTER® SERIES which will help you drastically shift your perception and open your mind to more self-reflection. You can learn so much about yourself, the way our bodies operate, and how our minds are amazing tools. You can choose what you desire to learn or be surprised by a "blind" book pick. Committing to new knowledge will help your brain develop in whole new ways, and the materials you implement in your day-to-day can actually change your life – or save it!

Will do ☐ on date: _____ Completed ☐ on _____

Reflect on how this changed or improved your life:

_____

> ## Novelty Tip #5:
> ### Skydive or try hang gliding.

If this freaks you out, take a deep breath! The statistics show that there is only 0.006 chance of a fatality occurring while skydiving solo, and only a 0.002 chance while skydiving tandem (with the instructor on your back). To put that into perspective, 1.3 million people die each year in car crashes, while another 30+ million are injured. Ready to take your chances?

Will do ☐ on date: _____ Completed ☐ on _____

Reflect on how this changed or improved your life:
_____

Friends you can invite to do this activity with:
_____

> ## Novelty Tip #6:
> ### Talk to strangers.

Start conversations with strangers without asking anything in return. Compliment them or ask them a question.

Will do ☐ on date: _____ Completed ☐ on _____

Reflect on how this changed or improved your life:
_____

> ## Novelty Tip #7:
> ### Try somewhere new for a romantic dinner out.

If you are in a relationship, go somewhere entirely new for dinner with your significant other. If you are single, put yourself out there by going somewhere new and not being afraid to sit alone! That level of confidence will have potential partners intrigued already. For more on this and how to increase your sexual energy, read **BE A MASTER® OF SEX ENERGY**.

Will do ☐ on date: _____ Completed ☐ on _____

Reflect on how this changed or improved your life:

_____

Novelty Tip #8:
Watch a scary movie.

Watch a scary movie with your significant other to get the blood and endorphins pumping. Studies show that being scared actually increases cardiac function and also endorphins. This activity seems to bond couples closer.

Will do ☐ on date: _____ Completed ☐ on _____

Reflect on how this changed or improved your life:

_____

Friends you can invite to do this activity with:

_____

Novelty Tip #9:
Go sing karaoke.

This works threefold: 1) you deal with your fear of public speaking or public shaming 2) you make yourself smile 3) you make other people smile. Life is too short; get up there and sing!

Will do ☐ on date: _____ Completed ☐ on _____

Reflect on how this changed or improved your life:

_____

Friends you can invite to do this activity with:

_____

> ## Novelty Tip #10:
> ### Play cards.

Learn a new card game or card trick and play with a friend or loved one instead of watching TV.

Will do ☐ on date: _____ Completed ☐ on _____

Reflect on how this changed or improved your life:
_____

Friends you can invite to do this activity with:
_____

> ## Novelty Tip #11:
> ### Do something you've never done.

Try a unique, fun experience like going to a roller derby, going to a paintball maze, or try laser tag. There are tons of options in most metro areas, but think of something you've never done. This expands the connections in your brain, gets your feel-good chemicals up, and keeps you young!

Will do ☐ on date: _____ Completed ☐ on _____

Reflect on how this changed or improved your life:
_____

Friends you can invite to do this activity with:
_____

> ## Novelty Tip #12:
> ### Go to the museum.

Go visit a museum, whether art, history, or science. You can even try the zoo or the aquarium. Read the plaques or take a guided tour, don't just walk through without soaking in the knowledge.

Will do ☐ on date: _____ Completed ☐ on _____

Reflect on how this changed or improved your life:
_____

Friends you can invite to do this activity with:
_____

> **Novelty Tip #13:**
>
> **Put on your party pants.**

Go to a thrift shop and find the craziest clothes you can; bring all your friends. After you've purchased your goodies, throw a thrift party or go out on the town. Not only do you support a great local cause, but you're also raising your vibrations and laughing with the people around you!

Will do ☐ on date: _____ Completed ☐ on _____

Reflect on how this changed or improved your life:
_____

Friends you can invite to do this activity with:
_____

> **Novelty Tip #14:**
>
> **Get crafty.**

Learn a new hobby, whether crocheting, screen printing T-shirts, or making birdhouses. Something to get your hands moving and doesn't involve a screen.

Will do ☐ on date: _____ Completed ☐ on _____

Reflect on how this changed or improved your life:
_____

Friends you can invite to do this activity with:
_____

> **Novelty Tip #15:**
>
> **Sleep outside.**

Go sleep in your backyard, balcony or even in the bed of a friend's truck. Spend the night looking at the stars and feel how small your troubles really are in the grand scheme of things. Be humbled.

Will do ☐ on date: _____ Completed ☐ on _____

Reflect on how this changed or improved your life:
_____

Friends you can invite to do this activity with:
_____

Personal Notes:
_____
_____
_____
_____
_____
_____
_____
_____
_____
_____

The Beginning – Not The End

After interacting with each step in this workbook, I hope you've taken a few things to heart:

1. You *can* be your most authentic self.

2. Change isn't as scary as you thought.

3. You control the outcome of your life.

So many people go through life thinking that the best college, the highest-paying job, or the fanciest new handbags are going to make them happy. They assume that they don't have control over their lives, or that they're just working until they can retire and finally *live*.

Now, I hope, you can see beyond that veil – the one that tells you there is nothing more to this life than stress, shopping, taxes, and TV. By now, I hope that you see the connections between your Mind, Body, and Spirit. I hope that you have taken great lessons away from this workbook, and that you are beginning to cultivate the truest YOU there is.

After all this time working on my own authenticity and my efforts to understand this extraordinary life, I have found ten things to be true:

1. There is an intelligent force guiding all we see… and can't see. Humans call this unseen force God, Universe, Jesus, Holy Spirit, etc. but it's all the same force, shown in many various forms. It is real.

2. We all have an invisible spiritual army of heavenly helpers at our beck and call 24/7, 365 days a year. They help us through our spiritual soul growth while we are here on Earth. A large part of society is unaware they have help from the other side, but everyone does.

3. We have the free will to choose to live this life without acknowledging the previous two points, and that is for our own life's journey or lesson.

4. We usually facilitate our supernatural sixth sense abilities after we put ourselves through very difficult times without awareness. In doing so, we grow ourselves spiritually, only to come to fully understanding and developing our power when we choose to look deep inside ourselves. We give ourselves our own issues to learn from.

5. Everything and everyone you knew, have met, or will ever meet are all connected.

Learning to see yourself in others, no matter how different they are, will give you compassion for others and yourself. This softens your judgement of others and brings love for your fellow human.

6. If you feel stuck or like life is unfair, you have chosen not to look deep inside to activate your God-self abilities and understanding. You choose to continue to experience the feelings, the challenges, the pain and difficulties to gain growth and experience in human form.

7. God (The Universe, the Holy Spirit, etc.) loves each and every creation formed, no matter its looks or its function. Everything matters to the Source Creator. Nothing is 'bad' or a mistake. All creations serve a purpose. If you do not consciously know your purpose, it is your duty to find out for yourself by doing soul work.

8. The weapons of manifestation to all things man could ever desire on this Earth are **'thought' directed by 'intention'** through an open, loving heart without doubt, judgement or criticism of self or others.

9. The world we see with our physical eyes is the illusion; the one we live when we dream is the true reality. We download information from the real "dream" world into this illusion to create and unfold a new perception of our human life.

10. Love is the only thing that is 100% real. All else is an illusion, including fear, grief, envy, jealousy, and pain experienced as the removal from love.

What have you learned thus far in your journey? What truths have you uncovered? It is my hope that this book will help you uncover your own ten truths, ones that guide you and lead to an unshakeable knowledge in your true self and purpose.

This may be the end of the book, but it's only just the beginning of your journey. To continue your personal growth and authentication process, check out the other books in the **BE A MASTER®** series; they will help you in more in-depth, evaluative, and powerful ways.

Conclusion

Thank you, dear reader, for picking up this book and working through it. We have taken a trip through activities that will open your horizons, ask (and answer) the hard questions, and help you decide what you desire in and from your life.

This book and the magic within has given you a chance to ask yourself what you desire for yourself, as well as shed a light on the process of thought creation through its pages. I hope you see now that your true, authentic self is just below the surface, waiting to step out into the world.

Refer to this book again and again throughout the next several months to a year as you tweak your desires. Revisit your In-Vision board collage pages and take the practices in this book seriously for your personal expansion. If anything, this book has given you a peek into your authentic, loving, and true self. With this knowledge, you can really tap into the joy and beauty of life.

There is, of course, much more expansion and many more steps that can be taken after you complete this workbook, and I hope you take full advantage of that opportunity by attending a live seminar. Here's to you... the real, lovable, authentically glorious you.

In the highest vibration of love and light, I want you to say, "I love my life" and REALLY mean it!

Theodoros Kousouli D.C., CHt.

About the Author

A holistic health care advisor, teacher, speaker, mentor and author who has been featured on major networks, Theodoros Kousouli D.C., CHt., is Los Angeles' premier holistic metaphysical energy healer. He is recognized and trusted for effective, quick, drug-free results, and his remarkable natural, pain-free, holistic healing system, the Kousouli® Method, focuses on getting patients to their top performance levels by unblocking pathways using the body's own repair mechanisms.

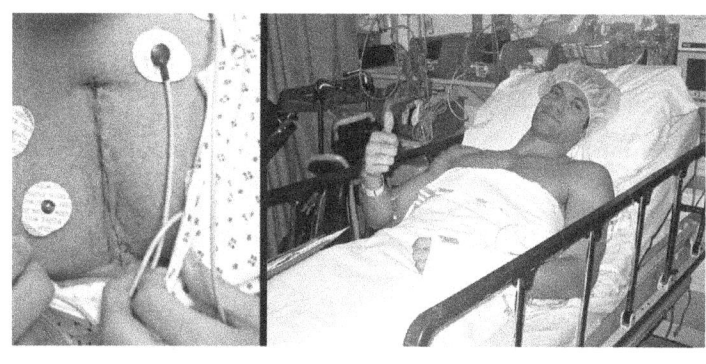

His desire to help others stems from his personal journey recovering from semi-paralysis and two major heart surgeries, and includes everything he's learned about the optimum wellness techniques that define his practice. Dr. Kousouli practices Hypnotherapy and Chiropractic care in private practice in Beverly Hills, CA.

Dr. Theo Kousouli is the author of the *BE A MASTER®* book series *(www.BeAMaster.com) including BE A MASTER® of PSYCHIC ENERGY and BE A MASTER® of SELF LOVE*. A personal coach and advisor to entertainers, business leaders, energy healers, and spiritual seekers of all varieties, Dr. Kousouli holds seminars teaching people how to tap into their inner healing and higher level abilities through the use of their nervous systems. Visit **www.KousouliMethod.com** and **www.BeAMaster** for more information on developing your intuition and personal power to live a more purpose-filled, meaningful, and healthy life.

Be a Master® of Your Reality

Life Changing Products · Books · Seminars · Empowerment Audios · Get on the Newsletter!

Connect with Dr. Kousouli, www.DrKousouli.com and on all Social Media Platforms

@DrKousouli #DrKousouli #KousouliMethod

You Will Also Enjoy Dr. Kousouli's Other Published Works Available Now from Major Retailers:

BE A MASTER® OF MAXIMUM HEALING
How to Lead a Healthy Life Without Limits
- Holistic Solutions for over <u>60</u> Diseases to Help You and Your Loved Ones Heal!

BE A MASTER® OF PSYCHIC ENERGY
Your Key to Truly Mastering Your Personal Power
- Uncover and Amplify Your Hidden Psychic Abilities to Change Your Life!

BE A MASTER® OF SEX ENERGY
Hypnotize Your Partner for Love and Great Sex
- Build a Stronger Bond with Your Lover(s) Using Subconscious Science!

BE A MASTER® OF SUCCESS
Dr. Kousouli's 33 Master Secrets to Achieving Your Dreams
- Solid Success Principles You can Apply Right Now to Empower Your Life!

BE A MASTER® OF SELF IMAGE
Dr. Kousouli's 33 Master Secrets to Living Healthier, Happier and Hotter
- Simple Holistic Tips & Tricks for More Weight Loss and Body Benefit to You!

BE A MASTER® OF SELF LOVE
Dr. Kousouli's 33 Master Secrets to Loving Your Extraordinary Life
- Overcome Bullying, Abuse, Depression and Build Massive Self-Esteem & Self-Love!

If you would like to share your story of how Dr. Kousouli's books, audios or seminars have impacted your life for the better, we would love to hear from you! (Messages are screened by staff and forwarded when appropriate.)

For A Free Gift from Dr. Theo Kousouli visit www.FreeGiftFromDrTheo.com

www.ingramcontent.com/pod-product-compliance
Lightning Source LLC
Chambersburg PA
CBHW080515110426
42742CB00017B/3124